VIDEO
MOVIES
WORTH
WATCHING

VIDEO MOVIES WORTH WATCHING
A Guide for Teens

David Veerman

BAKER BOOK HOUSE
Grand Rapids, Michigan 49516

Copyright 1992 by
Baker Book House Company

ISBN: 0-8010-9314-7

Unless otherwise indicated Scripture quotations are from the New
International Version, © 1973, 1978, 1984, International Bible Society.
Used by permission of Zondervan Publishers. Other versions used are the
Living Bible (LB) and the New American Standard Bible (NASB).

Printed in the United States of America

Contents

List of Reviewers

Robert Arnold
Executive Director
Metro-Maryland Youth for Christ
Baltimore, Maryland

Tim and Patty Atkins
Youth Ministers
Faith Baptist Church
Ft. Wayne, Indiana

Trent Bushnell
Executive Director
Greater Lansing Youth for Christ
Lansing, Michigan

Jack Crabtree
Executive Director
Long Island Youth for Christ
Dix Hills, New York

Robert Eugene DiPaolo
Assistant Pastor
Church at Charlotte
Charlotte, North Carolina

Kent Keller
Director of Singles Ministries
Key Biscayne Presbyterian Church
Key Biscayne, Florida

Mark Oestreicher
Junior High Pastor
Calvary Church
Santa Ana, California

Gary Schulte
Pastor to Youth
Evangelical Free Church
Grand Island, Nebraska

Janet Wielenga
Campus Life Staff
Greater Lansing Youth for Christ
Lansing, Michigan

Neil Wilson
Pastor
Eureka United Methodist Church
Eureka, Wisconsin

Len Woods
Pastor to Students
Christ Community Church
Ruston, Louisiana

Special thanks to
Claudia Gerwin
and Daryl Lucas
of The Livingstone Corporation.

Categorical Listing of Videos

Family Viewing

Anne of Green Gables/Avonlea
Chariots of Fire
Charly
The Chosen
Cry Freedom
Death of a Salesman
Driving Miss Daisy
Eleni
The Elephant Man
Fiddler on the Roof
Field of Dreams
Gandhi
Harvey
It Happened One Night
It's a Wonderful Life
The Journey of Natty Gann
The Mission
Mr. Mom
Mr. Smith Goes to Washington
Never Cry Wolf
The NeverEnding Story
Places in the Heart
Princess Bride
Rocky III
Stand By Me
Star Trek V: The Final Frontier
Tender Mercies
To Kill a Mockingbird
To Sir With Love
The Trip to Bountiful
The Wizard of Oz
Yentl

Junior High Age and Older

The Abyss
Amadeus
Big
The Color Purple
Dad
Ferris Bueller's Day Off
Footloose
The Fountainhead
Ghost
Home Alone
The Karate Kid

The Karate Kid Part 2
Kramer vs. Kramer
Les Miserables
Mask
The Money Pit
The Natural
On Golden Pond
The Outsiders
Rain Man
Roxanne
Witness

Senior High Age and Older

Absence of Malice
Cat on a Hot Tin Roof
The China Syndrome
Crimes and Misdemeanors
Dead Poets Society
Flatliners
King David
The Lords of Discipline
1984
An Officer and a Gentleman
One Flew Over the Cuckoo's
   Nest

Ordinary People
Papillon
Parenthood
A Place in the Sun
Presumed Innocent
Pretty Woman
Sophie's Choice
Terms of Endearment
The Verdict
Zelig

Introduction

When I was a child, I heard from preachers and other church leaders that movies were sinful and that Hollywood was a den of iniquity. Even Disney movies should be shunned, they said, because the money would help support the film industry. And so I avoided the movie theater like the plague.

Whether or not those well-meaning adults were right, movies have become a central part of our culture with a proliferation of media reviewers and conversations peppered with references to the latest films. And the questionable morality and values espoused cannot be so easily skirted by avoiding the theater. Television sets and VCRs bring movies right into our homes. And, ironically, during the past few decades as the moral standards of the film industry have dropped, most evangelical leaders have softened their stance toward Hollywood and its products.

Regardless of Hollywood in general and certain films in particular, clearly some movies are outstanding works of art and graphic portrayals of life. The cinema can be a powerful means of communicating ideas, evoking emotions, and motivating to action. That's why parents and youth workers should look for ways to let videos have a positive impact on young people.

In addition, films or parts of them can be effective discussion starters, tools for teaching biblical truth. And with the tremendous growth and availability of videocassettes, these films can be used in a variety of places. Parents can use movies to begin discussions with their children; youth workers can use film clips in their meetings.

As I said earlier, movies are intertwined inextricably in our culture, and kids love them. You'll get their attention when you talk in terms they can understand. We wrote this book to give you tools for ministry—in your family, in your neighborhood, or in your church.

The films were researched and the lessons written by men and women who work with young people every day—youth ministry veterans. They know the issues that kids are dealing with, and they know how to communicate with them.

How to Use This Book

The films have been arranged alphabetically; they have also been categorized according to suitability for three specific age groups—family (all ages but with parental approval), junior high age, and senior high age and older.

Nearly every lesson is divided into seven sections:

1. **Synopsis and Review:** a summary of the movie's plot and an evaluation of its quality.

2. **Suggestions for Viewing:** a quick look at ways of viewing the film to get the most out of it.

3. **Important Scenes and/or Quotes:** film highlights worthy of discussion.

4. **Discussion Questions:** a series of questions geared to understanding the issues raised and seeing them in the light of biblical principles.

5. **Outline of Talk or Wrap-up:** a summary of the biblical truths discussed and a challenge, especially for the youth worker.

6. **Related Bible References:** helps for further Bible study on the topic.

7. **Other Ideas:** additional ways to use the film.

Before you begin, however, remember that introducing a film to be discussed is almost as important as seeing the film itself. Young people are used to simply experiencing or seeing movies. Audiences today are seldom confronted with any question other than, "Did you like the film?" Few would expect to be asked to give thoughtful reasons for their liking or disliking a film. They need to be reminded to think and evaluate as they watch.

Watching and listening reflectively must be taught. If you are going to use videos regularly to spark discussion or to illustrate significant points, expect to run into frustration and limitations at the start. You may discover that the difficulties young people have in "getting anything out of Bible study" go far beyond that genre. Actually most kids find it difficult to get anything out of life.

If you can teach young people to think reflectively about the movies or music that they are somewhat interested in already, you will have moved closer toward their reflecting on the Scriptures and applying the truths they discover.

Your introduction of each video is vital for having effective discussions. Introductions prepare an audience, facilitate discussion, and focus attention on key points.

Finally, I should caution you about an important matter. What one person finds acceptable, another might find offensive. So be sure to preview the movies before you use them. Also, just because a specific film is included in this book should not imply a wholesale endorsement. Some movies are wholesome and helpful throughout, while others may contain only a worthwhile scene or two. We have tried to advise you of the content and warn you of any potentially offensive parts of each film.

I trust that you will discover a gold mine of invaluable information in *Video Movies Worth Watching.* May God bless you as you seek to communicate his truth to young people.

Dave Veerman

1
Absence of Malice

- PG
- 116 minutes
- A 1981 film

Synopsis and Review

Set in Miami, this 1981 drama centers around local businessman Michael Gallagher (Paul Newman) and his alleged involvement in the disappearance of union leader Joey Diaz. Gallagher's father had been a bootlegger and vehemently anti-union, so when the Feds come up empty in their search for those responsible for Diaz's disappearance, they turn their attention to Gallagher. The problem is, he's innocent, but that doesn't prevent them from pursuing the investigation and using the local paper (the *Miami Standard*) to make him look guilty. Megan Carter (Sally Field) is the reporter for the *Standard* assigned to write up the investigation. Predictably, she and Gallagher become romantically involved, and the plot thickens.

Along the way, there is considerable political intrigue and personal drama to make this a very engrossing movie. The acting is excellent, the plot is tight (if a bit complex at times), and the script is first-rate. *Absence of Malice* takes a direct look at the issue of freedom of the press vs. the individual's right to privacy. It doesn't give any real conclusions, but it certainly raises some valid, worthwhile questions.

Suggestions for Viewing

At just under two hours, you may be able to show this film in its entirety to your group without losing their interest. On the other hand, because the plot is somewhat intricate and there are no car chases, younger teenagers may have trouble staying with it. If you don't show the whole movie, I recommend the scenes described below.

Warning: there is some profanity and a suggested sexual situation.

Important Scenes and/or Quotes

1. Just over ten minutes into the film, Megan has a rather interesting conversation with the *Standard's* lawyer about law, truth, ethics, etc. It might be worth showing just for the issues it raises.
2. At approximately fourteen and one half minutes, Gallagher comes in to the *Standard's* office and confronts Megan about the story she's just written about him as the object of the Federal probe. Good stuff.
3. The most powerful segment of the film is the section from about forty-nine to sixty-five minutes, when Megan interviews Teresa (Melinda Dillon), Teresa commits suicide, and Michael confronts Megan over what she's done. It does an excellent job of displaying the power of the press in the lives of ordinary people—in this case, power for evil. This is raw, emotive stuff—especially Michael's confrontation with Megan—and needs to be used with discretion. But it will evoke strong responses.

Discussion Questions

As mentioned, the central theme of *Absence of Malice* is the tension between the right of the press to print information about people vs. those people's right to privacy. It is anything but a perfect balance, and raises a number of worthwhile questions:

Should the *Standard* have printed the first article naming Gallagher as the object of an investigation? If you were charged with making that decision, what would you have done?

When have you dealt directly with the mass media—TV,

radio, magazines, newspapers, etc.? How accurately did they report the issue or event?

Some of your kids may have parents or relatives in the media. Ask them to comment on some of the struggles reporters and writers face in their jobs.

When did a media investigation turn out to be a true benefit to society? (Hint—remember Watergate?) How about a time when the press went after someone unfairly? (Possibly your local media have done a hatchet job on some local church, pastor, or parachurch group.)

If you had been in Megan's position when Teresa revealed that Gallagher had been with her while she had an abortion—thus proving that he was innocent in the Diaz case—would you have printed the story? Explain.

How does *Absence of Malice* affect how you view the way the media reports the news?

Outline of Talk or Wrap-up

Say something like: "This movie does a good job of examining one of life's gray areas—the conflict between telling the truth and not hurting others unnecessarily. Megan's editor, Mac (Josef Sommer), makes the comment: 'I know how to print what's true; and I know how not to hurt people. I don't know how to do both at the same time, and neither do you.' That sums up the tension in this movie rather well.

"We all deal with this conflict at various levels—from telling someone we really like the ugly tie/sunglasses/whatever he or she gave us for our birthday, to parents figuring out how to break the news that they're divorcing to their children. The balancing act between truth and kindness can be very difficult.

"Paul writes in his letter to the Ephesians that 'speaking the truth in love, we are to grow up in all aspects into Him, who is the head, even Christ' (Eph. 4:15). There are three main elements prescribed here for honest Christian relationships: a) we have to speak it; b) it must be the truth; c) it must be spoken in love. Observing those three principles will help us maintain the balancing act."

Related Bible References

Matthew 5:1–16; Ephesians 4:15, 29–32; Colossians 3:8–17.

Other Ideas

Bring in someone from the news media (TV or newspaper) and ask him/her to discuss the problems of a free press in a pluralistic society like ours. If the person is a Christian, ask how he/she deals with the kinds of tension described in *Absence of Malice*.

Kent Keller

2
The Abyss

- PG-13
- 140 minutes
- A 1989 film

Synopsis and Review

The Abyss is a science fiction thriller drama about a research crew trapped on an underwater oil drilling rig. The crew, led by Virgil "Bud" Brigman (Ed Harris), is asked to help a group of Navy Seals inspect and destroy a damaged nuclear submarine. Joining them from the surface is Brigman's estranged wife, Lindsey (Mary Elizabeth Mastrantonio), who hates to be called Mrs. Brigman or even be associated with her husband. The crew's mission is to remove and defuse the nuclear warhead and destroy the submarine. During the procedure a hurricane on the surface cuts off their communication with the commanders directing the maneuver from the ocean surface.

The nuclear warhead, timed to explode in a few hours, is dropped into two and one half mile deep waters near the Cayman Islands in the Atlantic by a crazed Navy Seal (suffering from water-pressure induced psychosis). Bud Brigman volunteers to dive into the abyss (down 25,000 feet) to find and defuse the warhead. After successfully disarming the warhead, he runs out of air and is presumed dead. In the final scene an alien force that has been present throughout the adventure brings a revived Brigman and the entire damaged oil rig to the surface to be rescued.

Suggestions for Viewing

This is an exciting movie, worth watching in its entirety. If that's not possible, watch the last section of the film beginning with where Brigman leaves the underwater rig to dive into the abyss in search of the warhead. Watch until they are brought to the surface by the alien force and rescued. Caution: there is some rough language in this section.

Important Scenes and/or Quotes

When Bud Brigman dives into the abyss, Lindsey Brigman waits with the crew on the damaged underwater rig. She can communicate by voice with him, and he can type messages on a key pad back to her. In this life-threatening situation, Lindsey is finally able to express her feelings for Bud.

Although she has hated being called Mrs. Brigman, at this point, Lindsey senses the danger of the situation and begins to talk openly with her husband. "It's not until there is 10,000 feet of cold, black water between us that I can tell you how I feel," she explains.

After disarming the warhead, Bud has only five minutes of air left in his tank. He types back to Lindsey and the crew that he knew it was a one-way ticket. His last message is: "I love you, wife."

The crew hears nothing more from him. But then, when contact with the surface is re-established, and they pass on the bad news and plan their own rescue, they receive another typed message: "Virgil Brigman back on the air." He has been rescued by the alien force that eventually lifts the entire damaged rig to the ocean surface to be rescued.

It is important to note that Lindsey had voluntarily allowed herself to drown earlier in the movie when there was only one pressurized suit. Bud carried her body to the main station in the rig and revived her. She was willing to give up her life for him. Later he gave up his life to save the entire crew.

Discussion Questions

What would it take for you to give up your life for another person? Give an example of when that might occur.

What are some small ways you could make sacrifices (giving up some portion of your life) every week to help improve the lives of people around you?

Why were Lindsey and Bud only able to love each other when they were willing to give up their lives for each other?

When have you had a good talk with someone because of an extreme situation?

Why is it difficult for us to express our feelings to those we love?

If you knew someone in your family or a friend was going to die soon what would you tell him or her? Why can't you express that right now?

In what way is our communication with God hindered until we find ourselves in extreme situations? What has God done to open the doors of communication and relationship for us?

Outline of Talk or Wrap-up

Use this scene to uncover the broken communication we often experience with family members or friends. Use a personal illustration about an extreme situation in your life that opened opportunities to communicate with a fresh, new sense of honesty.

Emphasize the risk of waiting too long to talk with someone you love. Sometimes we have small arguments or fights that put permanent barriers in our lives because we are unwilling to admit when we are wrong or forgive the mistakes of another person.

Focus on Ephesians 4:26 (settling disputes quickly) and on Ephesians 4:32 (forgiving others just as Christ forgave us).

Challenge each person to write a short note to someone (parent, family member, friend or ex-friend) expressing what they would say if they were in an extreme, life-threatening situation. Ask them to deliver the note to that individual in person.

Related Bible References

John 3:14–15 (Jesus giving up his life so that all people will be brought together to worship him); Psalm 77 (in times of trouble, people seek after God); Psalm 70 (crying out to God for help); Colossians 1:21–22 (reconciled by Christ's physical death).

Jack Crabtree

3
Amadeus

- PG
- 158 minutes
- A 1984 film based on the life of Wolfgang Amadeus Mozart

Synopsis and Review

Winner of eight Academy Awards (including Best Picture), *Amadeus* depicts the rivalry between composers Wolfgang Amadeus Mozart (Tom Hulce) and Antonio Salieri (F. Murray Abraham).

The movie begins with a guilt-ridden Salieri, screaming, "Mozart, I've killed you!" and slitting his own throat. The suicide attempt fails, and Salieri is banished to an insane asylum. There, in a series of flashbacks, he angrily reveals to a young priest the reason for his bitter despair.

Salieri's lifelong dreams of glory (some for God, most for himself) have revolved around becoming a great composer. All his life he has devoted himself to chastity and hard work, hoping to achieve worldwide fame. Yet for all his efforts, he has managed only modest success.

The immoral and lazy Mozart, however, has become a household name. His compositions are brilliant masterpieces, "finished as no music is ever finished. Misplace one note, the music would be diminished. Misplace one phrase, the whole structure would fall apart. Here again was the very voice of God."

The longer Salieri ponders the great talent of Mozart (and his own mediocrity), the more consumed with envy he becomes. "Why would God choose an obscene child to be his instrument?" As far as Salieri is concerned, Mozart is nothing more than a "giggling, dirty-minded creature," an "unprincipled, spoiled, conceited brat." "If God didn't want me to praise him," the envious composer laments, "why did he implant the desire within me?"

Unable to come to grips with such injustice, Salieri at last renounces his faith and plots to destroy his rival. In disguise, Salieri commissions Mozart to write a death mass. His intention is to claim the mass as his own composition and to play it at Mozart's funeral.

However, the eccentric genius dies before he can complete the final composition. Mozart is buried in a pauper's grave, and Salieri is left to wallow in his envy, guilt, and mediocrity.

Suggestions for Viewing

Show the first ten and the final ten minutes of *Amadeus*. These scenes (dominated by Salieri's crackling dialogue with the young priest) are sufficient for your students to see the devastating effects of envy in a person's life.

The rest of this film (though beautifully filmed, and featuring elaborate sets and costumes) tends to drag.

Warning: *Amadeus* contains several lewd moments and a handful of vulgar remarks (almost all involving Mozart).

Important Scenes and/or Quotes

1. When Salieri finally, though reluctantly, agrees to talk with the priest, he tells of his desire to become a composer. During that scene (at the beginning of the movie) Salieri makes this eye-opening admission:

   I would offer up secretly the proudest prayer a boy could think of: "Lord, make me a great composer. Let me celebrate your glory through music and be celebrated myself. Make me famous through the world, dear God. Make me immortal. After I die, let people speak my name forever with love for what I wrote. In return, I will give you my chastity, my industry, my deepest humility every hour of my life. Amen."

2. When Salieri can no longer stomach the flawless talent of the godless Mozart and his own limited abilities, he consciously and willfully rejects God in prayer and announces his intention to destroy his rival:

From now on we are enemies. You and I. Because you choose for your instrument a boastful, lustful, smutty, infantile boy; and you give to me for reward only the ability to recognize the incarnation; because you are unjust, unfair, unkind, I will block you, I swear it. I will hinder and harm your creature on earth as far as I am able. I will ruin your incarnation.

Discussion Questions

What causes envy and how does a person overcome it?

Why do you think God gives such great talent and natural ability to people who don't even acknowledge or care about him?

What was wrong with Salieri's prayer as a child? (i.e. his prayer to become a great composer for God?)

What dangers lie in comparing oneself to others?

Put yourself in Vienna during the time of Mozart and Salieri. Assume both men are your friends. What could you say (what *should* you say) to each one about his attitudes and actions?

Outline of Talk or Wrap-up

Wrap up a discussion of *Amadeus* and the sin of envy by saying something like:

"You may not possess great worldly wealth, but if you know Christ, you are rich beyond comprehension (see 2 Cor. 8:9).

"Your name may not be famous the world over, but if you are a Christian, you are known by *God* (see 2 Tim. 2:19).

"You may not be the most talented person in the world, but if you are a Christian, then God has gifted you in a special way for a special task (see 1 Peter 4:10).

"So stop comparing yourself to others. Comparisons only stir up feelings of jealousy and envy. Focus, not on what you're *not*, but on what you *are*. Ask God to help you find out what it is that you do best. Then do that with all your heart, as God leads you.

"That's the way to find true contentment."

Related Bible References

Genesis 4:1–11 details the envy that Cain felt toward his brother Abel. Psalm 73 is the classic passage on the question of

"Why do evil men prosper?" Proverbs 14:30 says, "A heart at peace gives life to the body, but envy rots the bones." Proverbs 23:17 says, "Do not let your heart envy sinners, but always be zealous for the fear of the LORD." Proverbs 24:1 says, "Do not envy wicked men, do not desire their company." James 4:3 declares that prayers stemming from impure motives (like Salieri's above) are unanswered by God.

Other Ideas

Use *Amadeus* to discuss the fact that though we have been given different gifts (Rom. 12; 1 Cor. 12; Eph. 4; 1 Peter 4), no gifts are more important than others. Each of us has a crucial role in living for God and expanding his kingdom.

Len Woods

4
Anne of Green Gables

- Unrated
- 197 minutes
- A 1985 film

Anne of Avonlea

- Unrated
- 195 minutes
- A 1987 film

Synopsis and Review

These two Walt Disney movies, set on picturesque Prince Edward Island, Canada, presumably during the late 1800s, form an epic character study of relationships and growing up. They're *girl* movies (as boys would say). Not that boys won't enjoy the story of an orphan taken in by an elderly brother and sister. It's just that girls love watching, and secretly living, Anne's life.

Convincingly played by Megan Follows, Anne is a girl of extremes—she is either in total bliss or "the depths of despair." This is typical of the mood swings early adolescents face, and they enjoy seeing her triumph. As she wrestles to balance the pressures of her new home, maintaining her top-of-the-class standing at school, and shunning the romantic interest of a charming and ever-patient classmate, we see Anne develop a strong self-image and a genuinely pleasing outlook on life. The result is a young woman of conviction and optimism.

Suggestions for Viewing

Be prepared for some serious viewing time if you want to watch these movies! Each one consists of two videocassettes. That means if you watch both back-to-back, you're in for over seven hours of Anne. Oddly enough, that's the recommended viewing method. *Anne of Green Gables* stands on its own, but doesn't resolve the romantic issue. *Anne of Avonlea* continues the story without missing a step, and brings it to a wonderful conclusion. So start early—it'll be a late night!

Important Scenes and/or Quotes

Literally dozens of scenes in these two films would make excellent discussion starters. If you take the time to watch both movies you will find many you can use.

1. One great scene takes place about one half hour into the first film. Marilla (the elderly lady Anne is staying with) has asked Anne if she has seen a certain brooch. Anne confesses that she tried it on, but put it right back. With the brooch still missing, Marilla accuses Anne of lying and confines her to her room until she will confess stealing or losing the pin. While Anne is in her room, Marilla concludes that they will not be able to keep "a liar and a thief."

   On Marilla's next visit to Anne's room, Anne confesses losing the brooch in the lake. Shortly afterward, Marilla finds the brooch pinned on one of her own shawls. Taking the pin to Anne, she asks:

   > Whatever made you say that you took it and lost it?
   >
   > **Anne:** You said you'd keep me in my room until I confessed. I just thought up a confession and made it as interesting as I could.
   >
   > **Marilla:** But it was still a lie.
   >
   > **Anne:** You wouldn't believe the truth.

2. The second suggested scene near the beginning of the film follows the first by about ten minutes. It starts in the school room. A fellow classmate, Gilbert, calls her "car-

rots" (because of her red hair), much to her anguish. She breaks a slate over Gilbert's head.

Subsequently, Anne tells a friend she will never, ever forgive Gilbert for what he said. The following scene is hilarious, as Anne attempts to dye her hair black (it comes out green).

Discussion Questions

1. **Questions for the first scene**
What did Anne do that was wrong? Why?
Who was worse, Anne or Marilla? Why?
When are you tempted most to lie? Is lying wrong if someone won't listen to the truth? What if it will protect people?

2. **Questions for the second scene**
Why wouldn't Anne forgive Gilbert?
When have you held a grudge against someone?
What might make you say that you would never forgive someone?
If God's so forgiving, why is it difficult for us to forgive others?

3. **Questions for the whole movie**
Why is growing up such a pain sometimes?
When have your emotions been confusing?
With whom can you share your honest and real feelings? What does it take to get this kind of friend?
What are your dreams? What would you really love to do in life? Are those dreams worth sacrificing other good things? What things would you give up to reach your dream?

Outline of Talk or Wrap-up

1. Use the first scene to talk about honesty. After working through the discussion questions, be sure to present the biblical view of honesty. Stress that God is truth, and he can have nothing to do with falsehoods.
2. If you watch the whole movie, choose one or two topics

to cover—don't attempt to dig into every possible subject presented. The obvious overall topics are growing up, sacrificing your dreams for God's plan for your life, and forgiveness (it takes Anne one and a half movies to forgive Gilbert!).

Related Bible References

For the first suggested scene: Matthew 6:14–15; Romans 5:10; Colossians 3:13; Matthew 18:23-25.

For the second suggested scene: 1 Samuel 20:5-7; Jeremiah 38:24–27; Hebrews 6:18; Titus 1:2; Proverbs 24:26.

Other Ideas

One of the most creative ideas I've heard came from a junior high girl in Minnesota who invited nonChristian friends over for an Anne party. They dressed up in turn-of-the-century clothing and served raspberry slush. After watching both films with her friends (it was a sleep-over), she used the themes to present the gospel to her friends.

Mark Oestreicher

5
BIG

- PG
- 104 minutes
- A 1988 film

Synopsis and Review

Through the help of a strange arcade game (Zoltar), an adolescent boy, Josh Baskin (Tom Hanks), is transformed into an adult overnight. He quickly finds a niche in the toy business where he demonstrates an uncanny ability to know just what kids would like and dislike in toys. His naivete and exuberance are either captivating or threatening to the adults he meets. In the end, the hero does return to his childhood. In one of the poignant final scenes, he invites his girlfriend (Elizabeth Perkins) to go back with him. She responds, "I've been there already. It was hard enough the first time." The boy returns to a child's world alone.

One reviewer aptly described *Big* as "more a movie about childhood than a movie for children, the film's best audience would seem to be tired executives who long to act like kids." But there is another audience—a generation of teenagers who have grown up overnight, with little real experience of childhood. For one reason or another, they have been asked to put away childish things and take up adulthood before they were ready. Many parts of this movie express their experience.

Suggestions for Viewing

The movie is relatively tame and quite humorous. It is rated PG for implications about sexual activity. Most of the

sexual angle of the boy's brief adult experience is handled tastefully, but there is a short section of partial nudity in a scene
which implies that he and his girlfriend have sex. Dirty language is kept to a minimum.

This film is best viewed in its entirety and can be set up in a
group by using the following "starters."

Rocking chair pageant—Use teams and give each team an
assortment of outdated clothes from Goodwill, etc. If available,
include wigs, powder, and makeup. Have each team dress up a
boy and a girl to look as old as possible. Bring three or four cou-
ples in and have them role-play a panel discussion of rock
music from their characters' point of view.

Brainstorm the answers to the following questions as a possible introduction:

1. When you're 64, what do you hope to still have from
   your life right now?
2. Between now and 64, what are the most important
   things you expect to learn or gain?

Discussion Questions

After watching the film, ask the following questions:

What are the best parts of being a little kid?

What might be the best parts of being an adult?

Why do you think adults have such a hard time relaxing and
   being themselves?

Some people say that the hardest part about the in-between
   years is that young people are stuck between the world of
   kids and the world of adults. How well does this film show
   some of the problems of growing up?

How would you respond to the chance to skip over the next
   ten years of your life? What do you think it would be like
   to wake up tomorrow ten years older?

Jesus said we must come to him with a childlike faith. What
   was he referring to?

Outline of Talk or Wrap-up

Read aloud Matthew 18:1–5. Then make the following points.

1. To be like a little child is not to be childish, but childlike, displaying the best characteristics found in children. Some qualities of childlikeness (accompanied by clarifying questions) are:

   Curiosity/Questions—When you talk to God or read his word, do you ask questions?

   Spontaneity—Is what happens between you and God a set routine, or do you constantly discover his presence and activity in your life?

   Simplicity—Can you express, in clear and simple terms, your relationship with Jesus Christ?

   Faith/Trust—How long does it take for someone spending time with you to discover that you depend on Christ?

   Justice—Do you trust Christ enough to freely confess the sins you commit?

2. Apparently Jesus decided that if we were willing to be childlike with him, he could then teach us what it also means to practice adultlike attitudes with him. Childlikeness is the starting point. Which of these qualities above is lacking in your relationship with Christ?

Note—Invite students to ask Christ's help in developing specific areas. Pray with them and seek to follow up with study and conversation regarding those areas.

Related Bible References

Ephesians 4:14–16 (the difference between being infants and being "grown up"); Mark 10:14–15 (the importance of being childlike in one's relationship with God).

Neil Wilson

6
Cat on a Hot Tin Roof

- Unrated
- 108 minutes
- A 1958 classic based on the play by Tennessee Williams

Synopsis and Review

Cat on a Hot Tin Roof is the story of a dysfunctional Southern family whose members are forced to come to grips with their neurotic behavior. The family is ruled by the domineering patriarch Big Daddy Pollit (Burl Ives), whose impending death and sixty-fifth birthday have brought the family together on their 28,000 acre plantation in New Orleans. The family is comprised of Big Daddy's wife Ida/Big Mamma (Judith Anderson), his older son Gooper (Jack Carson), Gooper's wife Mae/Sister Woman (Madeleine Sherwood), a younger son Brick (Paul Newman), and Brick's wife Maggie (Elizabeth Taylor).

Big Daddy is an uninvolved father who, as Brick puts it, "built an empire, not a family." Gooper is the blindly obedient, yet unfeeling older son who has done everything Big Daddy ever asked him to do. Brick on the other hand is an immature, thirty-year-old former football player who uses alcohol to numb the pain of his disappointment. Mae and Maggie are manipulating "cats" who want their share of Big Daddy's estate. Mae attempts to use her five children and fertility to win Big Daddy's love; Maggie uses her good looks and keen sense of timing. Maggie knows what it means to be poor and isn't about to give up what she has managed to gain by marrying Brick. Unfortunately Brick is struggling with the effects of his dysfunctional relationship with his father, the suicide of his best friend Skipper, and the effects of alcohol. Consequently he refuses to give Maggie the one thing she most desperately wants—a child.

In the end Brick and Big Daddy reconcile their relationship. Brick and Maggie work out their differences. And both Brick and Big Daddy achieve a sense of personal redemption as they work through the pain, disappointment, and mendacity of life.

Suggestions for Viewing

This movie is suitable for viewing in its entirety. It contains no objectionable language nor scenes. While it does deal with the theme of human sexuality, and hints at the potential homosexual relationship between Brick and Skipper, it is not offensive or suggestive. This film, which exploits the complicated relationships within this Southern family, contains several powerful scenes that could be effectively used with a short plot summary. Below are a few suggestions.

Important Scenes and/or Quotes

1. Midway through the film, Big Daddy, Brick, and Maggie come to terms with how Skipper's death has affected Brick. In this sequence, Brick is forced to face the TRUTH about his crippling dependence on Skipper, his falsely blaming Maggie for Skipper's death, and the reality that he let Skipper down when it really counted. Brick asks, "How does one drowning man help another drowning man?"

2. At the end of the film is a wonderful exchange between Brick and Big Daddy in the basement of Big Daddy's house. Big Daddy has come to grips with the reality of his inevitable death and is wracked with pain that he refuses to numb with morphine. He says, "When you got it (pain) at least you know you're alive." Brick, who has come in from the rain where he symbolically broke his crutch (representing his crippling dependence on Skipper and alcohol), in the door of the car in which he was trying to escape, has come downstairs to confront Big

Daddy. They are surrounded by mounds of junk that Big
Daddy and Big Mamma have accumulated over the
years. Brick asks Big Daddy why they bought all this
junk. Big Daddy answers, "The reason a person buys
everything is because he thinks one thing he might buy
along the way is life everlasting, but you can't. One
thing you can't buy in any market on earth is your life.
You can't buy back your life."

Big Daddy and Brick engage in a dialogue concerning how
Big Daddy gave his family everything to prove his love. But
Brick tells him, "you can't buy love. I don't want things. I
wanted a father, not a boss." Then Brick says he doesn't know
what to believe in, there has to be some meaning, some purpose
in life. Big Daddy's account of his relationship with his
father—"the hobo"—spells out the value of love over the value
of possessions. While Big Daddy and Brick are coming to grips
with their pain, Gooper and Mae are upstairs battling with Big
Mamma for control of the plantation.

Discussion Questions

Why do we blame other people for our problems and difficulties in life? Brick uses alcohol to escape his disappointment
in life. How do you deal with your disappointment and
pain?

The way Big Daddy interacted with his family had many
grave consequences. Gooper became an unfeeling obedient
robot unable to think for himself. Brick became a rebellious
irresponsible alcoholic. How have your family relationships affected you?

Big Daddy put all his hope and trust in the accumulation of
wealth. In the end he realizes that all the money in the
world can't buy back missed opportunities. How should Big
Daddy have lived his life? What message does Big Daddy's
experience have for us?

What does Big Daddy mean when he says, "When you got it
(pain) at least you know you're alive"? How would pain
make you realize that you're alive?

Outline of Talk or Wrap-up

Cat has many excellent themes that could be used as discussion starters:

1. Coping with disappointment illustrated by Brick;
2. Unhealthy relationships illustrated by Brick and Skipper;
3. The impact of family relationships;
4. The importance of love; and
5. The transitory nature of wealth. Use the scenes described above and the Bible passages below.

Related Bible References

Psalm 49:6–19 (a psalm dealing with finding security in the accumulation of wealth, and riches' inability to save one's life); Matthew 7:24–27 (a parable about the necessity of building one's life on the proper foundation); 1 Samuel 18–20 (illustrating the healthy relationship between David and Jonathan); and 1 John 4:18 (the importance of love that drives out fear and covers sins).

Robert Eugene DiPaolo

7
Chariots of Fire

- PG
- 124 minutes
- A 1981 film

Synopsis and Review

Chariots of Fire tells the story of some of the events surrounding the 1924 Olympics in France. The careers of four young British athletes are compared and contrasted. Two in particular are featured: a Jew, Harold Abrahams (Ben Cross), who is determined to beat the anti-Semitism he encounters; and a devout Christian, Eric Liddell (Ian Charleson), who runs for the glory of God. Liddell, a child of missionaries in China, has his sights set on following his parents on the mission field. He struggles, however, with the tensions created by God's gift of world class speed. For Eric, his running is an intimate part of his relationship with God. At one point he says, "When I run, I feel his pleasure."

Richly deserving the awards it won as Best Picture, *Chariots of Fire* is rare in its attempt to deal with some spiritual issues. This film is entertaining and inspiring.

Suggestions for Viewing

Chariots is excellent entertainment for the whole family and may be viewed in its entirety. Here is a game that you can play with a youth group before viewing and discussing the film.

Zoo Relay—A race that can be run in a large space inside, or outside. Each team will have four competitors. Each "leg" will represent a different running style: elephant (runs holding a balloon between the knees and forming a trunk with both fists in front of the nose); ostrich (runs without bending the knees and with neck stretched out); rabbit (hops as quickly as possible); monkey (runs in a lope, bent over with hands handing down, almost brushing the ground); the baton is a banana that the monkey must eat after crossing the finish line.

Your introduction could include reference to the phrase, "The thrill of victory and the agony of defeat."

Important Scenes and/or Quotes

1. One scene (about one quarter of the way through) to watch carefully is the conversation between Eric and his sister on the mountainside when he explains why he wants to delay going to China as a missionary so he can run in the Olympics.
2. The scene in which Eric is put under great pressure by the British Olympic Committee to compete on Sunday which is against his convictions. (This scene occurs three quarters of the way through.)

Discussion Questions

Any of the following could be used as a focus for discussion.

1. *Why people compete*—Each of four British athletes (and two Americans) represents a different view of competition. For the Englishman of Jewish ancestry, Harold Abrahams, competition is the road to respect. For Aubrey Montegue, competition is fun and a little overwhelming. For Lord Lindsey, competition is great sport and entertainment. For Scotsman Eric Liddell, competition is a way to experience the joy of God's gift. The Americans are proven champions who also approach their craft in unique ways.
2. *The nature of convictions*—The most significant crisis in the film happens when Eric must decide whether or not to maintain his conviction that he shouldn't run on the Sabbath. Don't be surprised if young people have a difficult time relating to this as a problem at all. It is an

excellent point of departure for a discussion of whether or not they have any convictions.

3. *God's interest in the whole person*—Films dealing with spiritual issues tend to be lopsided, with characters appearing to be more religious than real. This story weaves the presence of God in Eric's life in a thoughtful and challenging way.

Use the following questions to discuss the film:

What is a conviction?

Which of these examples could be called convictions and why? (a) never narc (squeal) on a friend; (b) avoid pain at any cost; (c) don't ever let them see you sweat; (d) do unto others before they do unto you; (e) recycle; (f) the one who dies with the most toys wins; (g) Christians don't smoke; (h) just say no; (i) God loves me.

In what ways does the film show how Eric struggled to remain true to his convictions? What memories helped him? (He remembers telling a boy that the Sabbath is not a day for playing; he remembers that running is a means to achieve a greater goal.)

How do we get convictions?

When is the best time to examine what we believe?

How do we know if we really believe what we say we believe?

What impressions of Christianity could an open-minded person get from this film?

Why did *Chariots of Fire* win so many awards?

Outline of Talk or Wrap-up

Point out that at the end of the movie there's a note explaining that Eric Liddell became a missionary to China and then died during World War II in a Japanese concentration camp. Eric was a person true to his convictions, even when they cost him his life. Then make the following points:

1. Even if you don't agree with a person's convictions, you have to admire that person for standing by his or her beliefs.

2. Convictions can be right or wrong. What makes them convictions is that a person who has them holds them very tightly.

One of the themes of this movie looks at one man's conviction about how he ought to treat a special day. Explain that a lot of people, Christians included, might wonder what on earth could be so important about not running on Sunday. Some of the arguments used by those who were trying to convince Eric to run sounded pretty logical. We might even be tempted to mention Jesus' response when people tried to make too many rules about what you could and couldn't do on the Sabbath. Jesus said, "The Sabbath was made for man, not man for the Sabbath" (Mark 2:27). But the Sabbath (or Sunday) isn't about doing what we like to do (after all, Eric really liked to run); rather, it is about how each person answers the question, "How do I honor God in my life?" (Note: This might open the way for a series or a small group on personal discipleship.)

Point out that although the group members may think Eric's conviction was trite, they may not have one that is more worthy. Remind them that an unwillingness or fear to express a conviction makes it pretty weak. Without being overbearing, show students that making fun of another's convictions is often just a cover-up for not having anything we really believe in.

Give the following guidelines to help them consider and keep their convictions. If they can remember the word keep, they should be able to remember what you will tell them.

Know your convictions. Make a list of those things you really believe. Make sure you know or find some answers to the questions we've been asking during this session. Include everything you think might be a conviction. Ask others about theirs. If you want to start some interesting discussions, ask the question, "What would you be willing to die for?"

Examine your convictions. Take the list you've compiled and prioritize it. A conviction about dying for your country and a conviction that pizza is a minimum daily requirement are really in two separate categories, right? If you're doing this truthfully, you should end up with a short list of convictions. For a Christian, convictions can't violate God's word. The Bible is our most helpful tool for examining convictions.

Express your convictions. This is the action step in proving your convictions. If you can't tell others your convictions, they aren't convictions. They may be nice beliefs, but they aren't convictions. What we really believe, we live and express. So, if you ran into a lot of problems in the first two steps, take another look at the way you actually live. Those are your convictions. Is that really how you want it to be?

Preserve your convictions. You can expect to experience pressure when you go through the first three steps in developing convictions. If you've done your homework above, the pressure times aren't the times to try to figure out if you really believe your convictions. Pressure times are times to preserve, to persevere, to stand. If peer pressure or any other kind of pressure destroys a conviction, it wasn't really a conviction. Convictions are beliefs that stand up under pressure.

Close by quoting Paul's classic expression of personal conviction, Romans 8:38–39.

Related Bible References

Isaiah 40:26–31 (the passage Eric read in the church service while the races that he had chosen to miss were going on); Jeremiah 12:5 (obeying God in the little things of life); Colossians 3:17 (doing everything to the glory of God); Hebrews 12:1–2 (running the spiritual race with eyes on Christ).

Other Ideas

For more on Eric Liddell, see the book *The Flying Scotsman*. Also, Langdon Gilkey's book *Shantung Compound* includes a description of events surrounding Eric's death in a Japanese concentration camp during World War II.

Neil Wilson

8
Charly

- Unrated
- 103 minutes
- A 1968 film based on the novel *Flowers for Algernon* by Daniel Keyes

Synopsis and Review

Charly stars Cliff Robertson as Charly Gordon, a mentally retarded man whose night school teacher, Alice Kinian (Claire Bloom) befriends him. Alice persuades a clinic to perform experimental neurosurgery on Charly. The surgery is an outstanding success, and Charly becomes a genius. The movie follows Charly as he learns to handle the changes and challenges in his new life.

Although this movie is filled with stereotypes, it has profound comments on human behavior and is a sensitive study of a human being, showing how intelligence and emotions are intertwined.

Suggestions for Viewing

Charly is approximately an hour and a half long and is well worth watching in its entirety. It has many topics worth discussing, including the treatment of the mentally handicapped in our society and the value our society places on intelligence over other characteristics.

There is nothing offensive in the movie and it is suitable for viewing by all ages.

Important Scenes and/or Quotes

The following scene could be used to start a discussion on teasing or wisecracking. It takes place at the beginning of the movie while Charly is still mentally handicapped. He has a job sweeping floors at a bakery.

> **Baker 1**: Hey, Joe. Watch this. Hey, Charly. Charly! It's 5:00, Charly. Forgot what you have to do? (Charly looks puzzled.) Come on, Charly. Think. You were gonna take something home.
>
> **Charly**: Oh, yeah.
>
> **Baker 1**: For a minute there you had me worried. I mean you are always thinking such deep thoughts. How you gonna remember a little thing like your landlady's birthday?
>
> **Charly**: Yeah, Miss Apple's gonna be real happy and and and thanks for making me remember.
>
> **Baker 1**: What are pals for? Give me the broom. Me and the boys will help you clean up. (Charly starts to go to his locker.)
>
> **Baker 2**: Hey Gib, what gives?
>
> **Baker 1**: We filled his pail with raw dough this morning—full of yeast!

Everyone laughs and follows Charly. When he gets to his locker, there is bread dough seeping out. He is real puzzled. He opens the locker and starts pulling the dough out all over. Everyone crowds around and laughs at him.

> **Charly**: It growed. It got big.

Everyone laughs harder. Charly, unsure of what to do, laughs too.

Discussion Questions

Why do you think the men made fun of Charly?

In what ways do we make fun of people?

In what ways do we unintentionally make fun of people?

What are some of the reasons we make fun of people?

What does the Bible say about making fun of others?

What would Jesus have done if he were watching Charly's situation?

When have you stood up for someone who was being made fun of? How did you feel? How did those around react?

Outline of Talk or Wrap-up

This scene may seem exaggerated to some people, but we are all guilty of putting others down. Point out the line in the scene where the baker says, "You are always thinking such deep thoughts." That is a very subtle put-down. Explain the various ways we tease each other in the name of fun. Emphasize the real reason we do it—namely fear.

Talk about how the Bible instructs us to behave. Use Jesus as an example. People were drawn to him; they knew he would not put them down. As Christians, we are called to unconditionally love our neighbors. With God's help, we are able to set aside our fears and demonstrate a love that other people have never seen before.

Related Bible References

2 Timothy 2:25; Proverbs 16:18, 19:22; Colossians 3:12; Romans 12:16; 1 Peter 3:10–12; 2 Peter 1:7; Proverbs 11:17.

Other Ideas

In one of the final scenes, Charly learns that the experiment has gone horribly wrong and that he will either die or revert back to his mentally handicapped state. He confronts the scientists, accusing them of forgetting the human factor when they were doing their research. This could be excellent impetus for a discussion.

Tim and Patty Atkins

9
The China Syndrome

- PG
- 123 minutes
- A 1979 film

Synopsis and Review

The eerie thing about *The China Syndrome* is that it came out right before the incident at TMI (Three Mile Island), America's worst nuclear power accident. Since then, of course, we've had the disaster at Chernobyl, making TMI seem like a bad reaction in a child's chemistry set. If nuclear energy (and other technology vs. nature/ecology issues) is a concern to you and your group, *Syndrome* is a good way to launch into a sobering discussion of the issue.

The action revolves around reporter Kimberly Wells (Jane Fonda), a soft news, "fluff piece" type of reporter who happens to be touring a nuclear power plant with a camera crew when an *event* occurs—a serious problem in one of the nuclear reactors. The plant and the NRC (Nuclear Regulatory Commission) seem willing to sweep the whole thing under the public relations rug, but there are a couple of obstacles in their way. One is Wells and her cameraman, Richard Adams (Michael Douglas), who got the whole "event" (that is, the men in the control room's reactions to the event) on film. The other is Jack Godell (Jack Lemmon), shift supervisor on duty during the incident.

Jack is a loyal company man whose work is his life, but this episode causes him to do some serious soul-searching. His search leads him to the conclusion that this nuclear plant is unsafe and needs to be shut down. Of course, doing so would cost the plant and the energy company hundreds of millions of dollars and would be a PR fiasco as well. So all the powers that be combine forces against Kimberly, Richard, and Jack. Feeling that he has no other moral choice, Jack takes over the control room and goes on television, telling the public about the danger this plant poses to them.

As Kimberly is in the control room doing the interview, a SWAT team works feverishly to get in and take the control room back. Halfway into the interview, they succeed, fatally shooting Jack. As he lays dying on the floor, he gasps out the words, "I can feel it," meaning he feels the telltale vibration of another impending "event." The event passes without a meltdown (barely), but the message is unmistakable: this plant (and nuclear energy in general) is an unbelievably powerful time bomb that will go off somewhere, sometime.

Suggestions for Viewing

This is another film that unfortunately shows its age. The hairstyles and dress scream "late 70s!" If you and your kids can overlook that, *Syndrome* is a compelling drama. At just over two hours, you probably can use the whole thing. If not, here are some key selected scenes:

Warning: there is some profanity and violence (especially Jack's shooting).

Important Scenes and/or Quotes

1. Ten minutes into the movie you get the scene where Kimberly and Richard tour the plant. The next ten minutes or so, including the "event," are absolutely crucial to the story line.
2. At approximately one hour, there is a somewhat technical explanation of the phrase, "The China Syndrome." Because this is the movie's title, it might be helpful to watch that. Right afterward, we get to see the beginning of Jack's moral crisis, which is also pivotal.
3. The final half hour shows Jack taking over the control room, the climax, and the resolution (such as it is). It is gripping, and needs to be seen.

Discussion Questions

Nuclear power is a fact of life at this point in our country. Is this good or bad? Defend your point of view.

The reactors at Three Mile Island are still contaminated and shut down, and TMI wasn't even considered a major disaster. The Soviet report of the Chernobyl explosion listed 31 dead and over 200 injured. (The real figures are considered much higher.) What insights do these facts give you into the power of nuclear energy?

What would you have done if you were Jack, knowing that the reactor was unsafe, but also knowing that to take action would cost the company millions of dollars and cost you your job?

What obligation did the TV station have to broadcast the footage that Richard shot during the first event?

This movie is another study in the "technology vs. nature" vein. What can we do to alter our lifestyles so we use less electricity, thereby making nuclear power unnecessary?

How does our use of power and other natural resources relate to our faith in Christ?

Outline of Talk or Wrap-up

This movie shows us another area in which technology has gone beyond our moral ability to decide how to respond to life in the 1990s and beyond. (Other areas include artificial prolonging of life, genetic engineering, behavior modification, etc.) Life isn't getting any simpler; it seems necessary for us to formulate our moral principles as much as possible, in accordance with the Bible's teaching, and then seek to apply them to various areas of life, including our use of technology.

It is also important to remember that God has placed man as caretaker over his creation—we are responsible for how we discharge our responsibilities. This obviously means we are not to poison the air and land and sea (as happened at Chernobyl). It is unclear what acceptable levels of risk are as we seek to subdue the creation and make it work for us. That is an issue every one will have to resolve for himself or herself.

Related Bible References

Matthew 22:35–40 (How are we to love God first and our neighbors as ourselves in this technological world?); Genesis 1:26–31.

Kent Keller

10

The Chosen

- PG
- 108 minutes
- A 1982 film based on the novel by Chaim Potok

Synopsis and Review

During World War II Danny Saunders (Robby Benson) and Reuven Malter (Barry Miller) develop an incredible friendship even though their worlds are different. Danny is a Hasidic Jew (obvious by his dress and hairstyle) who is being groomed by his father, Reb Saunders (Rod Steiger), to become the next rabbi of his community, while Reuven is a Conservative Jew who loves jazz and piano and whose father, Professor David Malter (Maximilian Schell), is a secular scholar.

Together they explore one another's worlds. Danny, who has only studied Torah up to this point, sees his first movie, begins to read in other areas, and decides he wants to become a psychologist, while Reuven attends Hasidic Sabbath services, participates in a Hasidic wedding, and announces his intention to train to become a rabbi.

With the news that millions of Jews have been exterminated by Hitler, Danny and Reuven find themselves on opposite sides when discussions of a Jewish homeland arise. Danny's father believes only the Messiah can resettle the land, while Reuven's father refuses to wait and openly crusades for the partition of Palestine. Danny is forced to end their friendship but finally, when the state of Israel is formed, he and Reuven are able to reunite.

Suggestions for Viewing

The Chosen is a fascinating study not only in friendship but also in the customs of Hasidic and non-Hasidic Jewry. It is funny, heartwarming, provocative, and in no way offensive. Watch the entire film or the scenes described below.

Important Scenes and/or Quotes

1. One important scene occurs about three quarters of the way through the film. Danny and Reuven have not spoken for months. Reuven was excommunicated from Danny's family, and Danny obeyed and treated Reuven as if he were dead. After Israel becomes a state, the ban on Reuven is lifted. Danny finds Reuven studying in the library and approaches him and says hello.

   Reuven: I needed you and you weren't there.
   Danny: I'm sorry.
   Reuven: My father was sick, and it would have been nice if you were around.
   Danny: How is he?
   Reuven: He's better; he's home. Why did you do it?
   Danny: I had to. I chose to.
   Reuven: You might know how to live with silence. I don't.
   Danny: You learn how to live with it. You can hear the pain of the world in it.
   Reuven: You might, but I don't. I hate you, and I hate your father for what you did. It's sadistic.
   Danny: You hate me?
   Reuven: No, I don't hate you. . . . I'm glad you're back.

2. Another moving scene involves Danny and his father. Danny's father had decided not to talk to him, not because he didn't love him but because he did love him and he knew that Danny must be made to hurt or he would never be a good rabbi. In this scene Reb Saunders

explains to his son why he treated him with silence for all of those years.

Discussion Questions

Why was Danny and Reuven's friendship so strong? What factors kept them together while their worlds were so far apart?

If you were Danny and your father told you to stay away from your best friend, would you have obeyed? Why, or why not?

It was obvious how Reuven felt when their friendship ended; how do you suppose Danny felt? What must it have been like to have to treat a friend as if he were dead?

How would you have reacted in Reuven's place when Danny came back into his life?

What is your best friend like? If you had gone through what these two did, would you still be friends?

In what ways are you a good friend?

What characteristics are most important in a friend? How can a person develop these traits?

Outline of Talk or Wrap-up

Allow *The Chosen* to serve as an introduction to the subject of friendships.

Relate that good friends (those who endure in the midst of difficulties) are hard to find. Explain that we all want those types of friends but seldom are we willing to be that type of friend.

Encourage friendships that are based on the good of the other person even if that means they hurt more.

Related Bible References

Proverbs 17:17 (a friend loves at all times), 18:24 (a friend who sticks closer than a brother), 27:6 (a good friend hurts at times); John 15:13 (laying down one's life for a friend).

Other Ideas

The Chosen would be a good introduction for a discussion of father-son relationships. Each boy had a unique relationship with his dad. This movie would also be a good introduction to the traditions of the Jews and their understanding of the Bible and the Messiah.

Jared Reed

11

The Color Purple

- PG-13
- 152 minutes
- A 1985 film based on the novel by Alice Walker

Synopsis and Review

This is one of the great movies of the 80s. *The Color Purple* tells the true story of a black woman who grew up in the rural South. The details come both from a series of letters the woman wrote and diary entries addressed to God. *Purple* is really the story of three women.

The main character in *Purple* is a poor black woman named Celie (Whoopi Goldberg). As the movie begins, Celie becomes pregnant by her father and then must give away her child, as she had been forced to give away another child. Although Celie is abused by her father, she enjoys a close relationship with her sister, Nettie (Akosua Busia). Eventually Celie's father sells her to be married to a man named Albert (Danny Glover), whom Celie calls Mister.

Albert abuses Celie physically, sexually, and emotionally. He bosses her around, beats her, and generally treats her like a slave. Perhaps the most devastating hurt is his forbidding Celie to see Nettie again.

As if mistreating her were not enough, Albert brings home his mistress, Shug Avery (Margaret Avery), a nightclub singer and a woman with whom he has been in love for years. In the first encounter between the two women, Shug comments that Celie is as "ugly as sin." By this time in the movie, you can't miss the point: Celie is truly one of the poorest of the poor, living a life more oppressive and meaningless than most people could even imagine.

Ironically, it is Celie's relationship with Shug that ultimately gives Celie hope. Shug befriends her and becomes her inspiration to look for a way out of her desperation. The crucial scene takes place when Shug gets Celie to try on some of Shug's nightclub attire. Despite Celie's profound self-consciousness about her appearance, Shug gets Celie to look at her and smile. When Shug tells her that she has a pretty smile, Celie smiles widely and uncontrollably. For the first time in her life, someone has affirmed her. Her transformation has begun.

One of Celie's friends, Sofia (Oprah Winfrey), also has a reversal of fortune, but in the opposite direction. When we first meet Sofia, she is confident and self-assured. She does not tolerate the clumsy attempts of her husband, Albert's son, to be domineering. But when her headstrong ways clash with the mayor's wife, she is forced into servitude after spending time in prison. For years she does not even get to see her own children. Unlike Celie, Sofia's life goes from bad to worse.

Celie's final coming of age takes place at a gathering of family and friends around the dinner table. In response to Albert's abusive remarks, Celie talks back. Albert, though taken aback, tries to continue in his bossy manner, but Celie refuses to tolerate it. She knows who she is, and he is no longer able to control her.

Shug is the daughter of a minister, the prodigal daughter. She gave up singing in the choir to become a nightclub singer. Toward the end of the movie, when singing in a nightclub, she hears the sounds of the church choir, hears God calling, and becomes reconciled to her father.

The end of the movie is absolutely triumphant. Celie is seen running through fields of purple flowers; she is reunited with her children whom she has not seen since their birth, and with her sister (they are dressed in purple, the color of royalty). She also is given her own place in her father's will.

This story is taken right out of the cries of the psalmist. The oppressed live their lives wanting to know why they remain in oppression while the unrighteous continue to flourish. And yet, over the long run, it is the oppressed who are lifted up and the unrighteous who are crushed.

Suggestions for Viewing

The Color Purple is a very long, intense movie. It is well worth taking the time to watch, but it would not be realistic to view and debrief the whole movie in one sitting. Unless you have a lot of time (like at a weekend retreat), use selected segments.

There is some explicit language.

Important Scenes and/or Quotes

Purple has many great scenes that could be used for a number of different themes.

1. Segments (about halfway through) showing Celie's developing friendship with Shug would be useful in a discussion on self-worth. The focus could be on the proper way to develop a healthy self-image and how each of us can help others feel better about themselves by affirming them.
2. Celie's defiance of Albert at the dinner table (near the end of the film) could spark discussion on how to stand up to abusive people. It would be good to focus on what enables a person to have strength of character.
3. Shug's relationship with her father and the scene of their reunion (near the end of the film) would make an excellent starter for a discussion of rebellion and parent-child relationships.
4. Scenes from the end of the movie could also be used, with a proper introduction, in a discussion of how good ultimately triumphs over evil.

Discussion Questions

After watching the whole movie, ask:

Why does it appear that even very righteous people endure great suffering?

Why did Celie accept Albert's abuse for so long?

What do you think is the meaning of the title, *The Color Purple*?

Where in the movie do you see grace?

What transformed Celie's life?

How could Sofia have changed her life? Would she have been better off if she had submitted to the mayor's wife? Or was it good for her to stand up as she did and accept the results?

How can the effects of a poor parental example (like Albert for his son) be overcome?

Where do you see God in the movie?

What can we do to help people "blossom"?

Outline of Talk or Wrap-up

Read aloud Psalm 66:8–12. Then say something like:

"Celie's life is one of despair. From childhood her life seems destined for abuse, neglect, meaninglessness—a cycle she appears never to be able to escape. How can one life be so horrible?

"And yet somehow, some way, God's hand of redemption pulls her life out of the deepest pit and places her on a mountain.

"God does get angry when we see the color purple and do not rejoice. The color purple is one of majesty. It represents redemption. It is made up of red and blue. Red is symbolic of suffering. Blue is symbolic of death. And it is through death and suffering coming together that redemption is accomplished. It is in Jesus Christ's suffering and death that our deliverance occurs.

"Often we tend to view hard times as negative; rarely are we able to see in them the color purple. Often we feel that God has abandoned or is punishing us. We don't realize that often the hard times we face are a result of the fallen world we live in. And sometimes we fail to see that the goodness of God will bring redemption out of the suffering we are going through.

"*The Color Purple* reminds us that even in the deepest darkness there is hope in God!"

Related Bible References

God's grace—Ephesians 1:7–8; source of hope—Romans 5:1–5; 2 Corinthians 4:16–18; encouraging/inspiring others —1 Thessalonians 5:11, 14; suffering at the hands of evil people—Psalm 73; opposing/avoiding abuse—Nehemiah 6:1–9; overcoming the past—Ephesians 5:8.

Other Ideas

A meeting on how you deal with your enemies could be introduced with the segment where Sofia encounters the mayor's wife. Instead of submitting to the abuse of the mayor's wife, Sofia chooses to take a stand and as a result is forced into servitude.

Sofia and Celie could be used as illustrations of different ways to deal with abuse. It is particularly enlightening to look at the end results of each of their strategies.

Bob Arnold

12
Crimes and Misdemeanors

- PG-13
- 104 minutes
- A 1989 film written and directed by Woody Allen

Synopsis and Review

Crimes and Misdemeanors is an account of the lives of two men: Judah Rosenthal (Martin Landau), a successful ophthalmologist, and Cliff Stern (Woody Allen), a failed filmmaker. Throughout the film these men wrestle with the meaning and value of life as they attempt to sort through their respective worldviews.

Judah is involved in an affair with Dolores (Angelica Huston) that he wants to end. Unfortunately Dolores is unwilling to end the relationship. She threatens to tell his wife about them and disclose Judah's potentially questionable business practices. In desperation Judah turns to his seedy brother Jack (Jerry Orbach) to help him remedy his problem. Jack has Dolores murdered. The murder is blamed on someone else, leaving Judah free of both blame and Dolores. For the remainder of the movie, Judah attempts to come to terms with the guilt of his crime.

Cliff, whose greatest claim to fame is an honorable mention from a film festival in Cincinnati, is in the process of making a documentary film about a little known Jewish professor of philosophy, Louis Levy. Unfortunately Cliff is married to Wendy (Joanna Gleason) whose brother Lester (Alan Alda) is a major TV producer. As a favor to his sister,

Cliff Stern (Woody Allen, left) comforts Hally Reed (Mia Farrow, right).

Lester asks Cliff to film a documentary about his (Lester's) life for a PBS series. On the set Cliff falls in love with Hally Reed (Mia Farrow). Lester also falls for her. This leads to a contrast of character and consequences. In the end Lester wins out and is engaged to Hally, leaving a depressed Cliff to ponder the fairness of life.

Suggestions for Viewing

Crimes is a movie that could be shown in its entirety. It does contain some potentially offensive language and one questionable sequence early in the movie in which Cliff's sister describes her last date. At the same time there are several penetrating scenes that, with an explanation of the plot, could stand alone as excellent discussion starters. These are discussed below.

Important Scenes and/or Quotes

The themes running through this film concern the existence of God and justice in the universe. The phrase: "The eyes of God are on us always" is a recurring thought that plagues Judah as he struggles with his guilt. The most potent scenes are:

1. Rabbi Ben (Sam Waterston) visits Judah's office to have his failing eyes examined. Ben has come for a diagnosis, yet it is Judah who ends up asking him for advice concerning his problem with Dolores. This leads to a discussion in which Ben concludes that the fundamental difference between their two views of the world is that Judah sees the universe as harsh and empty of value, while he sees it as having a moral structure with some higher power who provides a basis by which to live.

2. In wrestling through his decision to have Jack get rid of Dolores, Judah imagines discussing this decision with Ben. The line to focus on is Judah's conclusion that "God is a luxury I can't afford." Ben responds, "What about the law? Without the law it's all darkness."

3. Scenes involving Judah's remembering conversations from his childhood connected by the theme the *eyes of God who sees all, rewarding the righteous and punishing the wicked* are also powerful. Toward the end of the movie, Judah visits his childhood home. There he recalls a Passover meal where his father Sal presented the view of the believer who trusts in God, even, if necessary, over truth. His Aunt May gave the view of the naturalist who rejects religion and faith in favor of realism where "might makes right." An uncle represented the nominal believer who is going through the motions only for the sake of tradition, but intellectually he didn't believe it. This is a powerful sequence that represents three worldviews colliding with one another.

4. *Crimes'* ending finds Judah (who has resolved his inner conflict by denying the reality of his guilt and is getting on with life) in conversation with Cliff whose life has fallen apart (Prof. Levy killed himself, Wendy is leaving him, and Hally is marrying Lester). The immoral, yet prosperous Judah is contrasted with moral, yet impoverished Cliff who is scandalized by Judah's fictional account of his crime.

Discussion Questions

Whose blindness, Ben's (physical) or Judah's (moral) is worse, and why?

What do you think Judah should have done? What do you do when confronted with the possibility of your sins being exposed?

Do you agree with Rabbi Ben that without the law (some absolute standard of right and wrong) all is darkness (there are no guidelines to tell us how to live)?

Which worldview do you agree with the most: Sal's, Aunt May's, or Judah's other uncle's? Explain.

In the end, Judah, who is guilty of murder, gets away with his crime while Cliff, who is only guilty of a few misdemeanors, loses his job with Lester, his project with Professor Levy, his wife, and Hally. How is it that those who do evil succeed and those who try to do what is right fail? Is life fair?

Outline of Talk or Wrap-up

Use the entire film or selected scenes to explore the question of meaning, value, and justice in life. How does belief (or lack of belief) in God impact a person's life? Discuss the concept of divine punishment for acts of wickedness and reward for acts of righteousness. Use this film as a springboard in the broader topic of worldviews and values. Show that without God, the universe would be cold, harsh, and meaningless, without any clear-cut standards of right and wrong. Contrast this with the clear biblical standards and the possibility of forgiveness found in the person of Jesus Christ when we violate these standards.

Related Bible References

Psalm 14:1 (the consequences of not believing in God); Proverbs 1:7 (belief in God as the beginning of wisdom); Ecclesiastes 1:2–11 (the meaninglessness of life apart from God); Ecclesiastes 12:13–14 (Solomon's conclusion about the meaning of life in light of the future judgment of good and evil); and Psalm 49 (a psalm that deals with the transitory nature of material success versus the eternal reward of righteousness).

Robert Eugene DiPaolo

13
Cry Freedom

- PG
- 157 minutes
- A 1987 film

Synopsis and Review

In this true story, Kevin Kline stars as Donald Woods, a white newspaper editor doing what he can to end apartheid in South Africa during the late 1970s. Denzel Washington is Stephen Biko, a leader in the Black Consciousness movement. Biko is a "banned" person because of his political involvement. This means he is never to leave his region of the country, nor can he ever be in the same room with more than one other person at a time. Biko's eloquent statements stress blacks seeing their own potential, rather than trying to overthrow the white government.

The movie helps the viewer see the struggle within Kline's character. How far should he go in his defense of Biko? How much should he jeopardize his family's safety to stand up against a corrupt system? As the movie progresses, Woods and his family are forced to escape from South Africa, leaving home and loved ones behind.

Cry Freedom wrestles with issues of race and culture and leaves the viewer without answers—which makes the movie more challenging than if its producers had spoon-fed us "the correct solution."

Suggestions for Viewing

Cry Freedom is lengthy—just over two and one half hours. Adults and older teens will have no problem with this. It's probably a bit long to show as a whole to a group of young teens, though a few of them would most likely enjoy it.

There are two scenes that could be shown on their own with minimal set-up. The first is a short dialogue on racism and the grid through which we see others and their views. The second discusses the concept of culture and ownership. Both are outlined below.

Cry Freedom is a clean film with little swearing.

Important Scenes and/or Quotes

Early in the film Donald Woods, the newspaper editor, first meets Steve Biko. After exchanging a few words, Biko refers to Woods as a "true liberal," to which Woods responds, "Not a title I am ashamed of, but one you obviously use with contempt." The conversation continues:

> **Biko:** I just think that a white liberal, who clings to all the advantages of his white world—job, education, housing, Mercedes—is, perhaps, not the person best qualified to tell blacks how they should react to apartheid.
>
> **Woods:** (smiling) I wonder what kind of liberal you would make, Mr. Biko, if you were the one with the job, the house, and the Mercedes, and the whites lived in townships.
>
> **Biko:** (also smiling) It's a charming idea!

The scene continues, and should be watched until Biko invites Woods to tour a black township with him.

The second scene is a speech given by Biko at a black soccer game, and can be found about one half hour into the movie. The core of his talk is below.

> We are going to change South Africa. But as angry as we have a right to be, we must remember that we are in this struggle to kill the idea that one kind of man is superior to another kind of man. And killing that idea is not dependent on the white man. We must stop looking to him to give us something. We have to fill the black community with our own pride. We have to teach our children black history, tell them about our black heroes, our black culture, so they don't face the white man believing they are inferior.

Discussion Questions

What feelings emerged as you watched this film? Why?

What makes people racist? Why would someone think their race was better than some other race?

What expressions of racism do you come into contact with in your school? How about in church?

If a shabbily dressed person of another race came into church on a Sunday morning and sat in the front row, how would people react?

Place yourself in one of the South African black townships, imagining you are a black teenager. How do you think you would react to Steve Biko's words? How would you react to the white government? How would your plight affect your relationship with God?

What is one thing you can do to help fight racism?

What do you believe in so strongly that you'd be willing to give up your home, friends, and country to stand up for it?

Outline of Talk or Wrap-up

Before showing any portion of the movie, distribute index cards and pencils and ask everyone to write down the race of the person that first comes to mind when they hear the occupations you read. Insist that they be honest and write their first reactions. Read the following list, pausing between occupations for response time.

cabdriver
shoe shine boy
banker
skycap
garbage man
convenience store night cashier
doctor

Be careful not to joke about these or you will perpetuate the very attitudes you're working against.

Explain to students that culture is learned. There is no part of our anatomy as a member of a certain race that makes us act or think a certain way, just like no one is born with an accent. Go on to discuss how God's Word is truth and is not given to any specific culture. Draw a picture of a man looking through a screen. Explain how we see God's truth through our cultural framework, just as people of another culture see God's truth through their cultural framework.

It might be fun to wrap this up by giving a few examples of how different cultures would interpret things we would consider normal. A missionary or anthropologist can help you find these differences.

Related Bible References

Galatians 3:28; Acts 10:34–35, 15:5–8; Jeremiah 13:23; Romans 1:14–17; Acts 10:9–23, 11:1–14.

Other Ideas

Have someone in your church come and speak with your group about what they had to give up to associate with Christ. This would be especially effective if you could get someone who has been rejected or ostracized by their family because of their faith.

Mark Oestreicher

14
Dad

- PG
- 117 minutes
- A 1989 film

Synopsis and Review

Dad is a moving story about the relationship between a father and son. It is a tremendous statement about where modern father/son relationships have gone.

Jack Lemmon plays the father, Jake Tremont. At the beginning of the film, his wife dies. Because Jake was totally dependent on his wife, he has a tough time adjusting to his new life. The son, John Tremont (Ted Danson), is a big city banker, who hasn't been home for as long as he can remember. This tragedy begins a new relationship between father and son.

Unfortunately, just as their new relationship begins, Jake discovers that he has terminal cancer. To meet his father's needs and to further develop their soon-ending relationship, John goes on leave from his job and returns to the small town to help his dad. In effect, John becomes parent to his father.

A new twist enters the story when John's son, Billy (Ethan Hawke) also returns to the small town to be with his father and grandfather. Billy decides to stay, but it soon becomes obvious that he and his father (John) will never have the quality of relationship achieved by John and Jake.

Dad is worth watching—it is a reminder of what should really be important in life.

Jake Tremont (Jack Lemmon, left) and his son John (Ted Danson, right) renew their relationship and enjoy a moment of pride in their accomplishments.

Suggestions for Viewing

Dad could be used effectively on a father/son weekend or evening. It would be worth viewing the whole movie although it might prove to be a very emotional time. With both fathers and sons present, death could become the dominant theme.

It is also possible to have a great discussion after viewing the scene described below.

You may also want to watch *Dad* together as a family.

The movie has some adult situations and explicit language so be sure to preview the film before showing it.

Important Scenes and/or Quotes

There is a scene where Jake and John talk about what the father wishes he could do over in their relationship.

For me, this is the most powerful scene in the movie. John and his father are talking about their lives together. Jake remarks that he wished he would have had more time for playing catch and just being with his son.

Discussion Questions

How to develop quality relationships within a family.

If you could relive your life with your parents, what would you change?

What do you wish you had more time for?

What do you need to do to improve your family relationships?

What is it that creates quality relationships between parent and child?

Outline of Talk or Wrap-up

If you use *Dad* with parents, focus on the necessity of spending time with their children and the importance of affirmation.

With teenagers, focus on what it means to develop a quality relationship with their parents. Explain that quality relationships occur when I

take responsibility for my life.

focus on listening to others.

spend time with others.

am willing to forgive even when I have been offended and when others are not sorry.

do what is right regardless of what others do.

Related Bible References

Exodus 20:12; Proverbs 10:1; Proverbs 17:6; Isaiah 45:10; 1 Timothy 5:4; 2 Timothy 3:2.

Other Ideas

Another way to use *Dad* would be to focus on the responsibility of children to their aging parents. A number of segments could be pulled from the movie, especially John's decision to take a leave of absence from his job to take care of his father.

Discuss the moral responsibility of children to care for their aging parents.

Bob Arnold

15

Dead Poets Society

- PG
- 128 minutes
- A 1989 film

Synopsis and Review

Dead Poets Society centers around the lives of several young men who are students at a prestigious prep school in Vermont called Welton Academy, and the impact made on their lives by one extraordinary teacher, John Keating (Robin Williams). Life at Welton is pretty much what you'd expect from an Ivy League prep school—rigid, demanding, and academic in the extreme. The main characters—Neil Perry (Robert Sean Leonard), Todd Anderson (Ethan Hawke), Charlie Dalton (Gale Hansen), Richard Cameron (Dylan Kussman), Gerard Pitts (James Waterston), Knox Overstreet (Josh Charles), and Steven Meeks (Allelon Ruggiero)—are wealthy, driven, and pressured boys trying their best to survive and excel, often seemingly more for their parents' egos than their own desires.

The principles that make Welton an excellent school —the "Four Pillars" as Mr. Gale Nolan (Norman Lloyd), the dictatorial headmaster calls them—are *tradition, honor, discipline, and excellence.* Life for the boys is pursuit of these worthy goals, until Mr. Keating arrives. He doesn't seek to negate or undermine these principles; he simply wants his students to see beyond the minutiae, the black and white, the sterility that often seems to be the end goal of academia. It is this clash of ideals—dry academics vs. creativity and freethinking—that gives the movie its tension and energy. *Dead Poets Society* is an excellent, thought-

69

provoking commentary guaranteed to stimulate some serious discussion of what's really important in life.

Suggestions for Viewing

Many of your kids may have already seen this movie and loved it. They will probably be glad to sit through it again. If you decide to just show part of it, however, I suggest the scenes listed below.

Warning: the film contains some profanity, so you may want to preview it beforehand.

Important Scenes and/or Quotes

1. At approximately two minutes forty-five seconds into the film, the "Four Pillars" are described. This is a brief scene, but it gives a good idea of what Welton is all about.
2. The best scene in terms of discussion-starting (Neil's suicide is the most powerful, but is such a bummer) comes at about ten minutes forty-five seconds to sixteen minutes fifteen seconds or so. This is where the boys first meet Mr. Keating in the classroom. He calls them out into a hallway, where the following discussion (in part) takes place:

Mr. Keating: "Seize the day". "Gather ye rosebuds while ye may". Why does the writer use these lines?

Charlie: Because he's in a hurry.

Mr. Keating: No. DING! Thank you for playing anyway. . . . Because we are food for worms, lads. Because believe it or not, each and every one of us in this room is one day going to stop breathing, turn cold, and die.

He calls them all over to the trophy case full of pictures of students from long ago.

They're not that different from you, are they? Same haircuts; full of hormones, just like you; invincible, just like you feel; the world is their oyster. They believe they're destined for great things, just like many of you. Their eyes are full of hope, just like you. Did they wait until it was too late to

make from their lives even one iota of what they were capable? Because you see, gentlemen, these boys are now fertilizing daffodils.
But if you listen real close, you can hear them whisper their legacy to you. Go on, lean in.
Listen—you hear it?
"Carpe . . ." Hear it?
"Carpe . . ."
"Carpe diem." "Seize the day," boys. Make your lives extraordinary.

3. One more very brief scene adds to this theme. At approximately twenty minutes, Keating and another teacher have a conversation about Mr. Keating's teaching methods and his philosophies. The punch line to the dialogue is Keating's line, "The powerful play goes on, and you may contribute a verse."

4. Neil's suicide is obviously a powerful and troubling scene. Show it and discuss it only with great sensitivity and much prayer. If any of your kids are suicidal or have attempted suicide, this scene will undoubtedly provoke some strong reactions. Be prepared to deal with the fallout. You may even want to have someone trained in dealing with suicide sit in with you.

Discussion Questions

This movie raises all kinds of powerful questions about the meaning of life, priorities, authority, etc. Ask:

What does the Welton Academy consider to be important? What do the boys' parents think? What do Neil, Todd, Josh, and the other boys think? Mr. Keating? How about you?

What do you think of the "Four Pillars"—*tradition, honor, discipline, excellence*? Are those worthy fundamentals? Are they sufficient?

With which characters did you identify? (Note: If someone says "Neil," it may be an important cue that there are serious emotional and/or psychological problems going on.)

Why did Mr. Keating make such a big deal over the Walt Whitman poem and the words, "Carpe diem?" What does that mean to you?

"The powerful play goes on, and you may contribute a verse." What does that say to you? What "verse" would you like to contribute?

Outline of Talk and/or Wrap-up

Say something like: "This movie makes a powerful statement about priorities, about the fragility of life. James 4:14 (NASB) says, 'Yet you do not know what your life will be like tomorrow. You are just a vapor that appears for a little while and then vanishes away.' We only have one life (Heb. 9:27) to live, and that of uncertain length. What do you want to accomplish with your life? What do you want to have written on your tombstone?

"The world says, 'He who dies with the most toys wins.' Jesus says, 'What does it profit a man to gain the whole world, and forfeit his soul?' (Mark 8:36 NASB). Choose which voice sounds like wisdom, and follow it."

Related Bible References

Psalm 90 (especially verse 10); Mark 8:34–38; James 4:13–17.

Other Ideas

It might be interesting to dig up some old yearbooks from the school(s) your kids go to, especially if they date back far enough that all or most of the people pictured are now dead. You could sort of recreate Mr. Keating's talk in front of the trophy case. Another angle on this (requiring some sensitivity) would be to gather pictures of the kids' ancestors. Either way, be careful not to cause unnecessary grief, especially in the case of someone's grandparent (for example) who may have died recently.

Kent Keller

16
Death of a Salesman

- Unrated
- 150 minutes
- A 1985 made-for-TV movie adaption of the play by Arthur Miller

Synopsis and Review

Willy Loman (Dustin Hoffman) is a traveling salesman whose life is in shambles. He wanted to be a traveling salesman because it was the thing to do in his day. Now, many years later, it is apparent that Willy has failed. He has one payment left on his house but is no longer able to go on the road to make a living.

Actually, most of Willy's life is an illusion. All of his great success is a figment of his imagination. Most of what was successful has been destroyed by a society that values productivity, which Willy has little of. Willy, as a salesman, built his route on his relationships. Now, his clients are more concerned with efficiency, and Willy is not able to compete.

Willy's two sons, Biff (John Malkovich) and Happy (Stephen Lang), lead the normal life of American boys. Their past heroics are constantly mentioned and are some of the illusions that keep Willy going.

When Willy approaches his boss about a move to the home office, he is fired from his job and told to rely on his sons.

Biff and Happy put together a plan to buy a sporting goods business. They too have lived their lives full of illusion. When Biff goes to a former employer to get a loan to start the business, the employer hardly remembers him. Their dreams are also shattered.

Willy's only remaining dream is that he is worth more dead than he is alive. He and Biff seem to reconcile. And Willy now realizes that his best move is suicide and he roars off to make the final profit—selling his life—so that he can get Biff on his feet financially.

Linda Loman (Kate Reid), Willy's wife, has the last word at the cemetery: "I can't understand it, Willy. I made the last payment on the house today . . . and there'll be nobody home. We're free and clear," she sobs. "We're free. . . ."

Suggestions for Viewing

This movie would be worth watching in its entirety as Dustin Hoffman gives a terrific portrayal of Willy Loman. And because it was made for television, there is very little that would be considered offensive.

Important Scenes and/or Quotes

1. *Death of a Salesman* is a story about choosing whether to build your life on truth or on illusion. Many students will be familiar with the story because of its use in literature classes.

   You could watch the whole movie or give an overview of the story and then watch the final scene. Then you could discuss how to face reality and come out on top.

2. After introducing the story line of *Death of a Salesman*, show the segment where Biff goes to his former employer and approaches him about a business loan. (This segment could also be used as an introduction to the above idea.)

3. A meeting or discussion could be developed around the importance of accepting our parents for who they really are. You could use Biff's and Happy's perspectives of their father as illustrations. Biff's time with Willy in Boston, where he realizes that his father is having an affair, could be very powerful.

Discussion Questions

Where did Willy Loman go wrong?

What made his life so frustrating?

How can you be sure that you are not living on unrealistic fantasies?

How can we face up to our failures and keep a strong sense of worth?

Outline of Talk or Wrap-up

Focus on Socrates' axiom that, "An unexamined life is not worth living."

At the heart of Willy Loman's failure is the fact that he did not come to grips with what was really happening in his life. For years he lived with a misconception of himself. He never had the strength to face himself truthfully. Eventually, this caught up with him and overwhelmed him.

An unexamined life is charging thousands of dollars on a credit card with no thought of future payment. But eventually that bill comes in the mail, and we have to face reality. It's important to face ourselves truthfully NOW and stop living the lie, pretending that we are something we're not and hoping that our problems will go away.

What are we like really? The Bible says we are not perfect, far from it. In fact, we are sinners, headed for hell—that's the bad news and it's reality. But the good news is that because of the forgiveness that Jesus Christ offers us, we can be forgiven.

Related Bible References

Matthew 6:14–15; Romans 3:23; Romans 6:23; 1 Corinthians 10:31; Colossians 3:23–24; 1 Timothy 6:6–10.

Bob Arnold

17
Driving Miss Daisy

- PG
- 99 minutes
- A 1989 film

Synopsis and Review

This movie addresses an issue that most people prefer to avoid—growing old. It became a hit greatly due to an Oscar-winning performance by Jessica Tandy as Miss Daisy Werthan, but also because it shows what happens when someone is unconditionally accepted, respected, and cared for.

In this case, the hero is a chauffeur named Hoke Colburn (Morgan Freeman) who faithfully serves Miss Daisy as she grows old.

When it becomes clear to Boolie Werthan (Dan Aykroyd) that his aging mother is no longer able to drive, he hires Hoke to be her chauffeur. At first, Miss Daisy wants nothing to do with Hoke. Eventually, however, she relents and allows him to drive her to the store, complaining all the way. *Driving Miss Daisy* follows the twenty-five-year relationship between this stubborn Jewish woman and her black chauffeur. At the end of the film, she states: "You're my best friend."

Suggestions for Viewing

This film is not too long, so you can watch it in its entirety. That way you will be able to see the development of the relationship between Miss Daisy and Hoke. If that is not possible, use the scenes described below.

Driving Miss Daisy is a particularly clean film and shouldn't offend anyone.

Important Scenes and/or Quotes

1. At the beginning, Miss Daisy wrecks her car.
2. At eighteen minutes, Hoke shows up for work but is not allowed to help. When Miss Daisy walks to the store, he follows in the car and is able to get her to ride with him (where she is a back-seat driver).
3. At forty-five minutes, Miss Daisy buys Hoke a gift so he can learn to write.
4. At one hour and three minutes, Hoke is rehired by Boolie with a raise to keep him from taking another job. Hoke says: "Ever have folks fighting over you? Sure feels good!"
5. At one hour and twenty minutes (to end), Miss Daisy is taken to a nursing home.

Discussion Questions

In our culture we rarely care for someone unconditionally, especially the aged. What elderly person(s) do you know, other than family? What could you do to make their lives a little brighter and better?

What about elderly relatives?

How can you apply the movie to the relationship you have with your parents?

Why was Hoke so loyal to Miss Daisy even though she mistreated him?

What do you think Hoke's feelings were toward Miss Daisy at the beginning of their relationship? after a few years? at the end of the movie?

What changed Miss Daisy's attitude toward Hoke?

Outline of Talk or Wrap-up

In our culture we can get so caught up in our own wants and desires that we take little time for others, especially the elderly. In fact we tend to ignore or make fun of them, just because they're old.

The truth is that older people are still people, invaluable creations of God, created in his image. So we should treat them as such.

In addition, older people are not "over the hill" and out of touch. They have much to offer us from their years of experience—wisdom, expertise, advice, and so forth.

Older people are often lonely—they need someone to be a friend, to talk to. And often they need someone to help with important tasks and errands (like driving).

Some older folks can be ornery at first (like Miss Daisy), but we shouldn't use that as an excuse to stay away. Instead, we should faithfully show love to them (like Hoke), as Christ's representative.

What older people do you know who need your attention and care? What can you do to show them Christ's love?

Begin by following through on one of the ideas we just came up with in our discussion. Better yet, try to extend your efforts to everyone you meet, including even the drive-through cashier at McDonalds.

You make a difference in the life of every person you come into contact with. Will you make their day a little better or a little worse?

Related Bible References

Matthew 7:12 (how will you want to be treated in old age?); Colossians 3:17 (we represent Christ); Luke 10:25–37 (the Good Samaritan showed unconditional care).

Trent Bushnell and Janet Wielenga

18
Eleni

- PG
- 117 minutes
- A 1985 film

Synopsis and Review

Eleni tells the dramatic, true story of a Greek mother's sacrificial love for her children.

Nicholas Gage (John Malkovich) is a *New York Times* reporter who is haunted by the torture and murder of his mother (the title character) at the hands of Communist rebels during the Greek civil war.

The movie begins about thirty years after that horrible crime, with Gage returning to Greece to track down his mother's killer. Through his investigation and the use of flashbacks, we discover the reason for Eleni's execution: she defiantly hid her children rather than let the communist authorities transfer them to Soviet satellite countries for re-education.

Eleni is an extremely powerful, must-see film.

Suggestions for Viewing

If at all possible, this film should be watched in its entirety. Not only is it good drama, but it also offers a glimpse of an important period in world history.

However, if that much time is not available, show only a couple of scenes: the ten-minute segment surrounding Eleni's execution, and the final scene where Gage decides not to take revenge on his mother's killer, but instead relates the lessons he has learned.

Eleni contains no sex and no rough language. There is one brief torture scene that may disturb some. Also, evangelicals may be troubled by a reference to Mariology. But do not let these minor points keep you from seeing this great film!

Important Scenes and/or Quotes

1. The most moving moment of the film occurs as Eleni faces the firing squad. A split second before her execution, Eleni raises her hands in triumph and yells, "My children!"

2. At the end of the movie, Gage makes the staggering statement:

   I am still mystified by the kind of love my mother felt for me and my sisters. The question of being worthy or not is no longer applicable. I accept it as something she gave me. I accept her love as my inheritance.

Discussion Questions

What is the significance of Eleni's cry at her execution?

What motivates an individual to suffer and perhaps even die for another person?

Imagine that someone has brutally killed your mother. Now imagine tracking that person down. You have a weapon and an opportunity to take revenge. What do you think you would do? Why?

Over time, how does bitterness affect a person? Why is it so difficult to forgive those who have wronged us?

The man who ordered Eleni's execution was the very same man whose life she had helped save some time before! What causes people to be so cold and vicious and ungrateful?

In what ways does Eleni remind you of Christ?

Outline of Talk or Wrap-up

The Mark of True Love

"My command is this: Love each other as I have loved you. Greater love has no one than this, that one lay down his life for his friends" (John 15:12–13).

"This is how God showed his love among us: He sent his one and only Son into the world that we might live through him. This is love: not that we loved God, but that he loved us and sent his Son as an atoning sacrifice for our sins. Dear friends, since God so loved us, we also ought to love one another. No one has ever seen God; but if we love each other, God lives in us and his love is made complete in us" (1 John 4:9–12).

True love, according to these passages, has three characteristics:

1. It sacrifices for others.
2. It pleases God.
3. It shows the world that we are Christians.

Related Bible References

Passages that talk about God's love and/or Christ's sacrifice on our behalf: Romans 5:8; Galatians 1:4; Galatians 2:20; Ephesians 5:2; Ephesians 5:25; 1 Thessalonians 5:10; 1 Timothy 2:6; Titus 2:14; 1 John 4:10.

Other Ideas

You could also use *Eleni* to discuss persevering under trial, the true nature of communism, or the importance of forgiveness.

Len Woods

19
The Elephant Man

- PG
- 125 minutes
- A 1980 film

Synopsis and Review

The Elephant Man is the true story of John Merrick, a man whose rare disease trapped him in a deformed body. His hideous looks were so bad that he was included in a freak show in a circus.

The film traces Merrick's movement from societal alienation toward societal acceptance. Eventually, Merrick (John Hurt) is able to move in high society, have tea with ladies, attend the theater, and build a scale model of a cathedral. These are incredible achievements for someone rejected as a freak, even considered by some to be cursed by the devil.

The Elephant Man is a heroic presentation of a man who overcomes a tremendous handicap.

Suggestions for Viewing

The Elephant Man should be watched in its entirety. Only when you see how terribly Merrick was treated at first can you appreciate his later acceptance. If time is a problem, however, you could show a short clip from the beginning to show Merrick treated like a freak and then show the scene where he meets with royalty.

Important Scenes and/or Quotes

The Elephant Man illustrates how we can live despite our weaknesses and imperfections. Stimulating discussions could follow either the whole movie or isolated segments (such as when Merrick recites Psalm 23 or when he meets with royalty).

Discussion Questions

How was John Merrick able to overcome his weaknesses and imperfections?

How can we learn to accept our weaknesses?

What should people build their self-worth around?

What is wrong with building your self-worth around your looks? Your athletic ability? Your intelligence? Your clothes? Your possessions?

What makes a person worthwhile?

How do we often react when we see people with extreme deformities?

What caused people to begin to accept Merrick?

How would Jesus have treated him?

How should we relate to deformed, handicapped, or "different" people?

Who can you think of that needs your acceptance and love?

Outline of Talk or Wrap-up

Begin by having each student write down three things that they see as their strengths. Then have them write down three of their weaknesses.

Talk about the bad ways kids try to build their self-esteem, some of which are self-destructive (e.g. winning at all costs, gaining acceptance through money, gaining "love" through sex, building a body through steroids, etc.).

Give them positive strategies for building self esteem—seeing ourselves as God sees us; spending time with people who bring out the best in us. (James Dobson's book, *Hide or Seek*, has a lot of good ideas on this topic.)

Explain how they can help others with their self-esteem, especially those who are shunned or rejected by society. And remind them that Jesus was rejected—He looked positively ugly to many (Isa. 53:2–3).

End with a time of affirmation where each member of the group says something positive about the other members.

Related Bible References

Exodus 4:11; Isaiah 53:2–3; Psalm 139:13–18; Romans 12:10.

Other Ideas

Have someone from your community who is disabled or hindered by a disability come and share with your group how they have learned to live with their condition.

Bob Arnold

20
Ferris Bueller's Day Off

- PG-13
- 103 minutes
- A 1986 film

Synopsis and Review

This 1986 movie smash takes a look at the life of a suburban high school senior, Ferris Bueller. Ferris (Matthew Broderick) fakes sickness to convince his parents, Katie and Tom Bueller (Cindy Pickett and Lyman Ward) and the school authorities (principal played by Ed Rooney) that he shouldn't be in school. He sets up an elaborate system to cover his tracks. During his day off, he has some amazing adventures in the city of Chicago.

The risks Ferris takes are fun and obviously foolish, like posing as someone else at a restaurant, using his best friend's dad's Ferrari, and devising a scheme to get his girlfriend out of school. Although *Day Off* is mostly light entertainment (the scenes of the principal trying to catch Ferris are hilarious), it does make a point—sometimes you need to take risks to realize what you are capable of.

Suggestions for Viewing

There is no need to show the complete movie. Start with the beginning and proceed until Ferris makes the statement: "Life moves pretty fast; if you don't stop and look around once in a while, you could miss it." (About the first ten minutes of the film). Discuss that section. Then show the last scene in the film, starting with Mrs. Bueller and Ferris' sister, Jeanie (Jennifer Grey), driving home from the police station. Finish with the final discussion questions.

If you have more time, show the clips of his day off in Chicago and delete the summarization after the second discussion question (see below).

Warning: for the most part this movie is quite mild, but there are bits of offensive language. Preview the scenes before showing them.

Important Scenes and/or Quotes

1. Ferris Bueller's statement: "Life moves pretty fast, if you don't stop and look around once in a while, you could miss it."

2. To introduce the second scene, say something like: "Ferris sets up elaborate schemes to cover his tracks. He convinces his best friend to let him drive his dad's Ferrari, gets his girlfriend out of school, poses as someone else at an expensive restaurant, crashes a parade and becomes the star of it. This next scene marks the end of Ferris's day off. He is trying to make it home before his parents get home from work. Unfortunately, his sister, who doesn't like Ferris because he always gets away with everything, runs into him and tries frantically to beat him home so her parents can catch him in the act." Show last clip.

Discussion Questions

What kind of a person is Ferris Bueller?

What is it about a person like Ferris that makes him so likeable?

With some close calls, Ferris makes it home safely and his parents are never the wiser for how he spent his day. All day long we see Ferris taking risks, stepping out of the norm. Describe a "Ferris Bueller" time you had where you didn't quite follow the norm. What were the results?

Ferris is a risk-taker. Which of his risks were good? Which ones were wrong?

What are some good risks that we can take to help others? change the world? do God's work?

What does Ferris mean by: "Life moves pretty fast, if you

don't stop and look around once in a while, you could miss it"? In what ways does your life move fast? What important events, people, and so forth might you be missing? What can you do to experience life more fully?

Jesus said that he had come to bring "abundant life." How might we miss the life he offers?

Outline of Talk or Wrap-up

Emphasize that sometimes we have to take risks to realize what we are capable of in different situations. If the men and women of the Bible had not stepped out of their comfort zone, the Gospel would not have been spread around the world.

We are willing to take risks physically—sports, musical instruments, mountain climbing; mentally—honors classes; socially—date, fall in love, make a new friend. But are we willing to take risks spiritually? Risk-taking for God involves trust in God. Trust in God = Belief + Action. If we say we trust God we must be willing to put that trust into action by reading the Bible and praying. It also means taking steps further in our relationship with God by doing a small group Bible study, learning to share our faith with others, and learning how to serve one another.

Colossians 3:17 (LB) states: "And whatever you do or say, let it be as a representative of the Lord Jesus." Encourage students to make the most of their junior and senior high school years.

Related Bible References

Hebrews 11 (study of men and women of faith); James 2:17 (faith by itself, if it is not accompanied by actions, is dead); John 15:12–13 (Jesus risked his life for us); study life of David, Elijah (specifically 1 Kings 18) and Esther.

Janet Wielenga and Trent Bushnell

21

Fiddler on the Roof

- G
- 181 minutes
- A 1971 screen adaptation of the Broadway musical

Synopsis and Review

This outstanding film spotlights the harsh life of a poor Jewish family in the Russian village of Anatevka in 1905 on the eve of the revolution.

Tevye (Chaim Topol) is a humble, hardworking milkman with five daughters. His life revolves around his Jewish faith and the numerous traditions that have been passed down from his forefathers.

Tevye reluctantly watches his three eldest daughters marry men of their own, rather than his, choosing. Tzeitel (pronounced Zight-ul) (Rosalind Harris) marries Motel (pronounced Moddle) (Leonard Frey) a poor tailor. Hodel (pronounced Huddel) (Michele Marsh) marries Perchik, an idealistic university student. In one of the film's most moving moments, she leaves her family to join her husband after he is arrested and deported to Siberia for anti-government activity against the Czar. Chava (pronounced Havah) (Neva Small) elopes with Fyedka (pronounced Fee-yet-ka) (Raymond Lovelock), a young soldier, who, most importantly, is *not* Jewish. For Tevye this third marriage is a violation of tradition and principle that his conscience cannot and will not allow. He turns his back on Chava.

At the same time as all this turmoil within Tevye's family, a government-sponsored persecution breaks out and the Jews are ordered to leave Anatevka.

As they sadly leave their beloved home, and as Tevye

and his wife Golde ponder their changing family and uncertain future, they trust God to guide and help them.

Fiddler on the Roof is a tremendous, life-affirming film!

Suggestions for Viewing

At one hundred eighty-one minutes (some versions were reissued at one hundred fifty minutes), this film probably cannot be viewed by your group in its entirety. However, by viewing the opening scene (which includes the song "Tradition") and perhaps the final fifteen to twenty minutes, students will get a feel for the changes that confront Tevye, his family, and his friends.

Important Scenes and/or Quotes

When Tevye makes a formal agreement that his eldest daughter Tzeitel will marry old Lazar (pronounced "Laser") Wolf, the town butcher, Tzeitel balks. She is in love with Motel, the local tailor. Motel explains to Tevye:

Motel: Times are changing, Reb Tevye. The thing is, your daughter Tzeitel and I gave each other our pledge more than a year ago that we would marry.

Tevye: (stunned) You gave each other your pledge?

Tzeitel: Yes, Papa, we gave each other our pledge.

Tevye: (looks at them, turns to the camera, sings)
[Reprise of the song "Tradition"]

> They gave each other a pledge.
> Unheard of, absurd.
> You gave each other a pledge?
> Unthinkable.
> Where do you think you are?
> In Moscow?
> In Paris?
> Where do they think they are?
> America?
> What do you think you're doing?
> You stitcher, you nothing!
> Who do you think you are?
> King Solomon?
> This isn't the way it's done,
> Not here, not now.

> Some things I will not, I cannot, allow.
> Tradition—
> Marriages must be arranged by the papa.
> One little time you pull out a prop,
> And where does it stop?
> Where does it stop?
>
> (Speaks) Where does it stop? Do I still have something to say
>   about my daughter, or doesn't anyone have to ask a
>   father anymore?

A similar scene occurs when Hodel and Perchik approach Tevye to announce their intention to be married.

When Hodel prepares to board the train to go to be with Perchik in Siberia, she sings, "Far From the Home I Love," to her father. The song includes these heart-wrenching words:

> Oh, what a melancholy choice this is,
> Wanting home, wanting him,
> Closing my heart to every hope but his,
> Leaving the home I love.

Near the end of the movie, Golde breaks the bad news to Tevye—his daughter Chava has married outside the faith. He is heartbroken, angry, and confused. Chava comes to him and the following exchange takes place:

> **Chava**: Papa, I want to talk with you. Papa, stop. At least lis-
>   ten to me. Papa, I beg you to accept us.
> **Tevye**: (to heaven) Accept them? How can I accept them?
>   Can I deny everything I believe in? On the other hand,
>   can I deny my own child? On the other hand, how can
>   I turn my back on my faith, my people? If I try to bend
>   that far, I will break. On the other hand . . . there is no
>   other hand. No Chava. No—no—no!

Discussion Questions

Would you enjoy having your marriage arranged by your parents—with the help of a local matchmaker?

What traditions in your family do you want to keep always? In your church?

What traditions or values of your parents or your church do you feel you might not follow? Why?

Is it possible for man-made traditions to (wrongly) become more important than God's commands?

Imagine being the parent of a beautiful little girl. You have watched this little one come into the world. You have loved and protected her. Cared for her. Provided for her. Cried over her. Laughed with her. Prayed for her. Under the very best circumstances, it would be difficult to see her leave your home. Now imagine that your precious little girl wants to marry someone who will take her far away from you. Worse, suppose she wants to marry a man with radically different religious beliefs. How do you think you might react?

Was Tevye wrong to turn his back on Chava? Why or why not?

How should children's relationships with parents change once they marry?

Are there any spiritual values or beliefs you would be willing to:

—die for?

—turn your back on your family for?

—forsake your friends for?

Outline of Talk or Wrap-up

Solid Faith in a Shaky World

If we want to stand strong in an ever-changing world, we must anchor ourselves to God and his unchanging Word (Mal. 3:6; Heb. 13:8). That involves at least four things:

1. Evaluating our human traditions in light of God's inspired word (Mark 7:1–13).
2. Knowing and doing the clear-cut commands of Scripture (James 1:22).
3. Developing convictions for all those unclear areas of life.
   "Does it help me?"
   "Does it control me?" (1 Cor. 6:12)
   "Does it hurt others?" (1 Cor. 8)
   "Does it glorify God?" (1 Cor. 10:31)

4. Living consistently with all we believe (Rom. 14:21) regardless of the consequences (Luke 9:23; 57–62).

Related Bible References

Luke 14:26 records the words of Christ, "If anyone comes to me and does not hate his father and mother, his wife and children, his brothers and sisters—yes, even his own life—he cannot be my disciple." This verse can be used if you choose to use *Fiddler on the Roof* to discuss values and beliefs that should never be compromised. Matthew 15:1–6 and Mark 7:1–13 feature Christ's rebuke of the Pharisees because of their greater devotion to traditon than to God's Word. Use Genesis 2:24 and Matthew 19:5 to discuss the important but difficult step of sons or daughters making a break from their parents when they marry.

Other Ideas

Use *Fiddler on the Roof* to launch a discussion on dating (i.e. how it is a Western, twentieth-century practice).

Len Woods

22
Field of Dreams

- PG
- 106 minutes
- A 1989 film

Synopsis and Review

> Ray, people will come . . . they'll come to Iowa, they'll
> come as children . . . longing for the past . . . they'll pay.
> For you see that it is money they have and peace they
> like. Just like when they were children, they'll sit in the
> bleachers on a warm afternoon, cheer their heroes, watch
> the game and dip themselves in magic waters. . . .
> America has rolled through the centuries like a steam-
> roller, built and rebuilt again. But baseball has been the
> constant! It has marked the time. It is a part of our past. It
> reminds us of what was once good and what could be
> good again.

Such were the words of Terrance Mann (James Earl
Jones) at the height of the movie, *Field of Dreams*.

America is in need of rootedness, and movies are con-
tinuing to use themes that meet that need. A number of
movies suggest that baseball is the one distinctive
American tradition. *Field of Dreams* is one of the best.

As Ray Kinsella (Kevin Costner), an Iowa farmer, is
standing among the stalks of corn in his field, he hears a
voice, "If you build it, he will come." When he doesn't
understand the spoken message, he gets a vision of a baseball diamond that is to be built right there in his cornfield.
If he builds it, he believes, Shoeless Joe Jackson (Ray Liotta)
will come and play on it. Shoeless Joe was an infamous
member of the 1919 Black Sox, banned from baseball for
deliberately losing a World Series game.

Like anyone who has a vision, Ray has to go out on a limb to realize it. He nearly loses his farm to bankruptcy. He travels to Boston to enlist the support of Terrance Mann, a famous author from the 60s, to help him carry it out. After these steps of faith, the miraculous takes hold, and his dream becomes reality.

Suggestions for Viewing

To fully understand *Field of Dreams*, you probably need to see the whole film. On the other hand, you will be able to have a good discussion by using the scenes described below.

Warning: there is some offensive language.

Important Scenes and/or Quotes

1. Although you don't realize it until the end, the central theme of *Field of Dreams* is the relationship between Ray and his father. Ray's father wanted Ray to play baseball, but Ray didn't, and they drifted apart. Eventually, Ray's father died with the relationship still estranged. As it turns out, Ray's becoming reconciled with his father by fulfilling his father's dream is what this film is all about.

   Begin with an overview of the movie to help to put the discussion in proper perspective. Use the part where Ray talks about this unfulfilled dream as a discussion starter on the relationships between a father and his children. Also show the scene at the end where Ray and his dad are reconciled.

2. Another possibility is to watch the whole movie and focus on the cost of fulfilling a dream.

Discussion Questions

Why did the voice want Ray to build the field?

Who was to come?

What does the title *Field of Dreams* refer to? Whose dreams were fulfilled in that field?

What role does a father play in the lives of his children?

What dreams do your parents have for you?

What causes parents and children to fight and hate each other? Why do we tend to hurt the ones we love?

What can you do to heal the relationship with your parents?

What does the Bible say about our relationship with our parents?

When does "obeying" stop? When does "honoring" stop?

Outline of Talk or Wrap-up

Encourage students to make the most of the days they have with their parents. Challenge them to become a positive part of their family by honoring their parents. Tell them to discuss unfulfilled dreams with their parents.

Explain that when we are under the direct authority of our parents (we're minors and living at home), we are to obey them unless they tell us to disobey God. When we grow up and move away, we no longer have to do what they say. On the other hand, we never outgrow our responsibility to honor our parents. This means treating them with respect, listening to their advice, caring for them in their older years, and so forth.

It's true that sometimes parents have unrealistic expectations for us, putting us under a lot of pressure. But parents also understand us better than anyone else, so their counsel is invaluable. Unfortunately, however, we often reject what they say and rebel against their authority. Only when we're older do we realize how wise they were . . . but then it's too late.

Don't let youthful stubbornness or a foolish argument come between you and your parents.

Play the Mike and the Mechanics song, "The Living Years." Its message is that we often wait until it's too late to express our feelings to those we love.

Related Bible References

Exodus 20:12; Ephesians 6:2–3; 1 Corinthians 13.

Other Ideas

Talk about the cost of fulfilling a dream. Use Moses as an example of someone who paid a price to carry out a dream (Exod. 3:1—4:17). Ask:

Whenever a person has a dream, do you think it is necessary for him or her to go out on a limb to make that dream happen?

How can you know if a dream is worth pursuing?

To be successful in carrying out a dream, what does a person need to do?

Describe one of your dreams. What will it cost to carry it out?

Use Luke 14:28–33 (the importance of counting the cost).

Bob Arnold

23

Flatliners

- R
- 111 minutes
- A 1990 film

Synopsis and Review

What happens to a person after death? Five medical students (including Kiefer Sutherland, Kevin Bacon, and Julia Roberts) who have been asking that question attempt to find out. With the help of drugs, each in turn "flatlines" (becomes brain-dead) to explore what lies on the other side.

From the reports of several patients interviewed, the students expect to find love, security, and protection. Instead, each comes face to face with someone they have hurt in the past. When they are revived (brought back to life) those people (or at least the memories of them) return with them, seeking revenge. It is only when they ask for forgiveness from the ones they have hurt that they find peace.

Flatliners asks the right questions. The students probe the subject of life after death (centering on sin, forgiveness, and even God) but conclude that even science does not provide the answers they are seeking.

Suggestions for Viewing

Christians should see *Flatliners*. Although it is rated R (and deservedly so), the subject matter is superb. This box office hit deals with important questions that people are asking. Though it offers no answers of any substance, the fact that it asks insightful questions is enough.

To be useful in a church setting, much of the film could

(and should) be edited. All of the important scenes can be condensed to less than forty-five minutes.

Important Scenes and/or Quotes

1. The first shot of the movie is of Nelson (Sutherland) looking out over the water. As he raises his hands he shouts, "Today is a good day to die!"

2. Rachel (Julia Roberts) is determined to "die." No one wants her to be part of the experiment but she insists.

   Fabracio: Why are you doing this?
   Rachel: Look, I've lost people that are close to me. I just want to make sure they're in a good place.
   Fabracio: There's something I didn't tell you about last night. I had this feeling that if I had gone any farther that there was something out there protecting me, something. . . .
   Rachel: Good? . . . Are you trying to tell me the atheist now believes in God?

3. When Nelson flatlines for the second time, the others try to revive him and cannot. It looks as if he will stay dead.

   Fabracio: It's not fair and it's not right. I'm sorry, God, that we stepped on your . . . territory! Isn't that enough?

Discussion Questions

What important questions did *Flatliners* address? What were the students' answers to each question? Were you satisfied with their answers? Why or why not?

What does the movie propose happens when a person dies?

How do you think the characters in the movie would define sin? How did each person attempt to "atone" for his or her sin? Do you agree?

Where would God fit into their understanding of death and sin? Is God seen as good or evil?

What happens to a person who dies without being forgiven for his or her sins?

What does the Bible say about sin? How can a person get forgiveness?

Do you think it is helpful or harmful for a person to watch a movie like this? Why or why not?

Outline of Talk or Wrap-up

Allow *Flatliners* to help you introduce the subject of sin. (Though the movie centers around death, it is more concerned with what happens after a person dies rather than death itself.)

Stress that the Bible is clear in what it states about sin. Though *Flatliners* understands sin to be any wrong done against another (whether actual or perceived), the Bible has a different focus. When we sin, it is the heart of God that breaks.

State that forgiveness has more to do with restoring our relationship with him than with asking forgiveness of those whom we have offended (even though that may be appropriate too). Therefore, death will not consist of people seeking revenge for the evil we may have done them, but will center on a holy God who can tolerate no sin.

Explain that *Flatliners* could offer no satisfactory conclusion because God was left out. Anytime that God is forgotten, the results will be the same.

Make clear that God does offer the forgiveness for which the medical students searched but that it comes through Jesus Christ.

Related Bible References

Hebrews 9:27 (die and then face judgment); Romans 5 and 6 (death to sin as master); Psalm 51 (sin is against God), 130:4 (forgiveness from God); Colossians 1:14 (forgiveness through Jesus).

Other Ideas

Flatliners would also be useful to begin a talk on death itself (including "life after life" experiences) in an attempt to formulate what the Bible says. It could also stimulate thinking in the area of medical ethics.

Jared Reed

24
Footloose

- PG
- 106 minutes
- A 1984 film

Synopsis and Review

The sound track for *Footloose* features several chart-topping tunes of the mid-80s. The movie takes place in a town where rock music and dancing have been outlawed, mostly on the insistence of Ariel Moore's (Lori Singer) father, the Reverend Shaw Moore (John Lithgow). The new kid in town is Ren MacCormack (Kevin Bacon), who has moved there with his recently divorced mother. Ren loves rock and roll and wants to help his new classmates have a dance. This endeavor does not mix well in a town that is dead set against rock music. The movie centers around Ren's efforts to have a dance.

Suggestions for Viewing

Footloose will be most helpful if you view specific scenes and then discuss them. The movie tends to cast a negative light on religion, features teen rebellion, and has some swear words. However, *Footloose* contains some classic parent-teen encounters, both positive and negative. These key scenes can serve as discussion starters.

Important Scenes and/or Quotes

Explain that this film takes place in a town where rock music has virtually been outlawed. Then show the drive-in scene near the beginning. Stop when Ariel's father sends her home. Then show the scene later that night when Ariel attempts to apologize to her father. Stop at the end of this conversation.

Discussion Questions

Where do you see yourself in the apology scene?

In what ways can you see your parents—how would they react? (Ariel tries to apologize; Dad is cold, Dad won't stop and listen; Ariel wants to challenge the music rules but doesn't.)

Move ahead to where Ariel comes home well after curfew. Her father has been waiting up for her. Pause after this confrontation between Ariel and her father. Before punching the play button, divide the group in half. Have one half watch for attitudes or statements of Ariel's they have thought or said themselves. The other half should look for attitudes or lines their parents have said. Afterward, have the groups share their observations.

Ariel
yells first
wants to be accepted for who she is
resents suspicion
Dad
restricts friendships
is suspicious
is worried about what other people will think

Point out that the next scene is an example of good communication skills between parent and son. In this scene Ren and his mother have a heart-to-heart talk about Ren's desire to have a dance. Ren has gotten a lot of flack trying to buck the system. (You may want to apologize for a swear word in the dialogue!) This time have the guys watch for what Ren does to help the communication and have the girls watch for what his mom does to help the communication. Afterward, have the groups report their observations.

Ren
becomes vulnerable and opens up
keeps talking, doesn't stop
tells her what's on his mind
Mom
asks questions
is available to talk
sits down
encourages Ren to talk
listens carefully

Ren has come to ask Ariel's father if he can take her to the dance. Show the scene that ensues between Ariel and her dad. Stop at the end of the dialogue. Beforehand, explain that this is a good example of communication. Have the guys watch for good things dad does, and have the girls watch Ariel.

Dad
admits that he doesn't have all the answers
finally meets Ren
listens
Ariel
compliments her dad
says she knows he has a tough job

The final prom and dance scene is fun to watch.

Outline of Talk or Wrap-up

Review the barriers to communication that were illustrated in *Footloose*. List additional barriers (e.g. busy schedules, resorting to name-calling, reminding of past mistakes, etc.). Point out the *communication enhancers* seen in the movie. Add other ideas (e.g. not assuming the worst, being trustworthy, being willing to take a risk, etc.).

Explain that love and respect should be the key ingredients in any relationship, but especially in parent-teen relationships. Remind them that they cannot control the other person's behavior—they can only control their own behavior and responses. They must be responsible for their own actions. Change can only occur if they change how they act.

Related Bible References

1 Corinthians 13 (the love chapter); Colossians 3:17, 20 (the importance of obeying parents), Ephesians 6:1–4 (instructions for kids and parents), John 13:34–35 (love is a commandment).

Gary Schulte

25
The Fountainhead

- Unrated
- 114 minutes
- A 1949 film based on the novel by Ayn Rand

Synopsis and Review

Howard Roark (Gary Cooper) is an architect who stands alone. Rather than kowtow to bosses, the idealistic Roark takes a job busting quarry rocks while he designs and plans original buildings. Rather than permit the construction of a drastically altered housing project that he designed, he blows up the project. When brought to trial, he accepts no defense but his own. This movie is a tribute to everyone willing to stand by what's right, no matter what the cost.

Because of the 1949 production date, there is a very dark, heavy-handed feel to the movie. Also, because this movie is based on the book by Ayn Rand, much of what is said is extremely humanistic. However, there are great scenes worth using to point out man's need to stand up for what he believes.

Suggestions for Viewing

Fountainhead is worth viewing in its entirety. There are no special effects or flash, but there is terrific acting, with Patricia Neal as Dominique, Gary Cooper as Howard Roark, and Raymond Massey as Gail Wynand.

Fountainhead is suitable for all audiences, but be aware that the humanistic approach may provoke strong reactions from viewers.

Important Scenes and/or Quotes

Roark is brought to court because of damage to the building he designed. He offers only this thought-provoking defense that earns him an acquittal.

Thousands of years ago the first man discovered how to make fire. He was probably burned at the stake. He taught his brothers to light, but he had given them a gift they failed to see. And he lifted the darkness off the earth.

Throughout the centuries, there were men who took first steps down new roads armed with nothing but their own vision. The great creators, the thinkers, the artists, the scientists, the inventors stood alone against the men of their time. New thought was opposed. Every new invention was denounced. Men of unborrowed vision went ahead. They suffered and paid, but they won.

No creator was prompted by a desire to please his brothers. His brothers hated the gift he offered. His truth was his only motive. Work his only goal. HIS work, not those who used it. HIS creation, not the benefits others derived from it. The creation which gave form to truth. He held his truth above all things and against all men.

He went ahead whether others agreed with him or not. With integrity as his only banner, he served nothing and no one. He lived for himself and by living for himself, he was able to achieve the things which are the glory of mankind. Such is the nature of achievement.

Man cannot survive except through his mind. He comes on earth unarmed. His brain is his only weapon. But the mind is an attribute of the individual. There is no collective brain. The man who thinks must act on his own. The reasoning mind cannot work through any compulsion. It cannot be subordinated by the needs, the opinions, or wishes of others. It is not an object of sacrifice.

The creator stands on his own judgment. The parasite follows the opinions of others. The creator thinks, the parasite copies. The creator produces, the parasite loots. The creator's concern is the conquest of nature. The parasite's concern is the conquest of man. The creator requires independence. He neither serves nor rules. He deals with men by free exchange and voluntary choice. The parasite seeks power. He wants to bind all men together in common action and common slavery. He claims that man is only a tool for the use of others. That he must think as they think. Act as they act and live in selfless joyless servitude to any need but his own.

Take a look at history. Every great achievement has come from the independent work of some independent mind. Every horror and destruction came from attempts to force men into a herd of brainless souls. Robots without personal rights, without personal ambitions, without hope or dignity.

It is ancient conflict. It has another name. The individual versus the collective. Our country, the noblest country in the history of men, was based on the principle of individualism. The principle of man's inalienable rights. It was a country where a man was free to seek his own happiness, to gain and produce, not to give up and renounce. To prosper, not to starve. To achieve, not to plunder. To hold his highest possession a sense of personal value. And his highest virtue his self respect.

Look at the results. That is what the collectivist is asking you now. To destroy as much as the earth has been destroyed.

I am an architect. I know what is to come by the principle on which it is built. We are approaching a world in which I cannot permit myself to live. My ideas are my property. They were taken from me by force, by breach of contract. No appeal was left to me. It was believed that my work belonged to others to do with as they pleased. They had a claim upon me without my consent. That it was my duty to serve them without choice or reward.

Discussion Questions

What individuals can you think of whose ideas have been pirated?

How responsible should people be to society's ideals?

Why is society so demanding of its creators, artists, etc.?

How demanding are we of ourselves when it comes to standing up for what we believe?

When have you had to stand alone?

How do you think Jesus would respond to Roark's speech?

What parts of Roark's speech sound like Jesus? What parts do not?

How would you define righteous anger?

When is aggression all right?

When does God expect us to be individuals? When should we be part of a group?

Why does God want more than a group of individuals to serve him?

When was the last time you experienced "suffering silence"?

Outline of Talk or Wrap-up

Give examples of original thinkers, artists, creators who were either ripped off or attacked (Gandhi, van Gogh, Spielberg, etc.). Explain how society has prospered at the expense of a few leaders who gave what they had even though the reward wasn't adequate. Talk about the difference between a thermometer and a thermostat. One sets the temperature, the other is the indicator or follower.

Talk about Jesus' desire that we stand alone with a strong faith. We should look to society to give cues for areas of service. Jesus wants us to lead the masses into serving him and each other. You may want to use this quote by Henri Nouwen: "By looking at society critically and wanting to sacrifice for the good of others, we lose the lone ranger attitude and gain the pleasure of God. The last individual act."

Related Bible References

Romans 12:1–3; Romans 8:29; Hebrews 13:16; Proverbs 15:8.

Tim and Patty Atkins

26
Gandhi

- PG
- 188 minutes
- A 1982 film

Synopsis and Review

Gandhi is a tremendous portrayal of Mohandas K. Gandhi (Ben Kingsley), who is known to most people today by his spiritual title, Mahatma Gandhi. The film spans his life from his early days as an attorney fighting prejudice in South Africa to his later days as India's spiritual and political leader. It shows us who he was by picturing his nonviolent protests in India's early history, first from British imperial rule over India, and then from the conflict between Hindus and Muslims within India.

Suggestions for Viewing

There are a number of ways to use this film. You could show it in its entirety. For those students willing to sit through its 188 minutes and serious themes, the exposure to a man of such strong moral conviction will be a rare treat. After seeing the film, you can then discuss what made Gandhi so unique and effective as a leader.

Another good use of the film would be to discuss Gandhi's commitment to nonviolence, especially in protesting the problems of his day. Before showing any of *Gandhi*, give a short history of white colonial rule in India and how Gandhi came to believe in nonviolent response. Then show the segment where Gandhi's followers walk peacefully toward a line of British soldiers, only to be beaten to the ground by those soldiers.

Discussion Questions

Why do you think Gandhi's belief in nonviolence helped in India's struggle against imperial Britain?

Why do you think Gandhi's belief in nonviolence failed to resolve the nation's internal conflict between the Hindu and Muslim peoples?

What made Gandhi unique?

What did Jesus mean by, "Do not resist an evil person" (Matt. 5:39)?

What did Jesus mean by, "I did not come to bring peace, but a sword" (Matt. 10:34)?

What kinds of problems and situations are you against in our society?

How can you protest against them, nonviolently?

What can you do to heal conflicts between individuals?

Outline of Talk or Wrap-up

1. Issues of war and nonviolence have a long history of discussion in the Christian community. Rather than trying to debate them here, it would be better to focus your discussion on Gandhi as a person of conviction. He had an ideal and he stuck to it. He kept his eyes focused on a small set of goals and relentlessly, single-mindedly pursued them. What can we learn from him?

2. You could also discuss Jesus' teaching about turning the other cheek and returning good for evil. So often we want to respond to personal insults and wrongs by fighting back and hurting the other person. Instead, we should think about how Jesus would respond in that situation, and we should do what is most loving and Christ-like.

Related Bible References

Genesis 6:11 (the earth is full of violence); Matthew 5:38–42 (turn the other cheek); Matthew 26:52 (those who live by the sword die by the sword); Luke 6:27–36 (love your enemies); Romans 12:17–21 (don't take vengeance or return evil for evil); 1 Peter 3:8—4:19 (suffering for doing good).

Other Ideas

You could take the section where the movie focuses on Gandhi's simple life, especially his use of the spinning wheel, and discuss the value of living a simple life. Then you could ask:

How has materialism made our lives easier?

How has materialism made our lives more difficult?

How could a person in our society be happy living the way Gandhi did?

How could we live more simply?

Bible references for a simpler lifestyle include: Matthew 6:24 (don't love money); 1 Timothy 6:6–10 (the love of money leads to all sorts of problems).

Bob Arnold

27
Ghost

- PG-13
- 127 minutes
- A 1990 film

Synopsis and Review

Ghost is a comedy, a drama, a love story, and an action film all in one. Patrick Swayze (Sam Wheat) and Demi Moore (Molly Jensen) give strong performances but Whoopi Goldberg (as the spiritual adviser Oda Mae Brown) shines.

Sam works in a bank and lives with Molly, an artist. After finding a total of 11 million extra dollars in several of his accounts and raising questions as to its source, Sam is murdered by his best friend Tony. Tony, another banker, tired of his salary and eager for the good life, is the one who has been stealing the money and has secretly stashed the money in Sam's accounts hoping no one would notice. But he resorts to murder when his embezzling is discovered. Unknown to Tony, however, Sam had wisely hidden the codes necessary to access the accounts.

When Sam dies he doesn't go to heaven or hell like most people. Another ghost explains to him that he was taken before his time and since he was murdered, he is allowed to remain on earth to avenge his murder. No one can see him, but Oda Mae (who up to that time had been running a scam operation for those who wanted to communicate with the dead), can hear him.

As Tony tries to woo Molly to find the missing codes, Sam, with Oda Mae's reluctant help, desperately tries to protect Molly from also being killed by Tony.

Eventually, after Sam is avenged and Molly saved, the money is given to charity, and Sam travels to heaven.

Suggestions for Viewing

Ghost is an enjoyable movie. There are a few adult situations and some rough language but the movie could be watched in its entirety.

The three scenes involving death could also stand alone. They graphically depict what happens to a person at death; those who are evil are escorted to hell by demons while those who are good walk toward the light to heaven.

Important Scenes and/or Quotes

1. Tony dies near the end of the movie. As he dies, his soul leaves his body. Sam is also there and Tony begins to talk to him, but demons come, grab the frightened man, and delightedly howl as they drag him away.
2. The last scene involves Molly and Sam. Finally she can see him (though he is dead). As they talk, a beam of light appears from heaven. "They're waiting for you, Sam," says Molly. Sam tells her that he loves her and adds, "It's amazing, Molly. The love inside, you take it with you." Then he walks into the light and is gone.

Discussion Questions

What happens to people when they die? Do they become ghosts?

How do you know if there really is a heaven and a hell?

Can you really talk to someone who has died?

What determines whether a person goes to heaven or hell?

How would you answer if someone asked if you were going to heaven or hell? How can you be sure where you are going?

Why do you think God would set heaven and hell and how to get there?

Outline of Talk or Wrap-up

Use the short scenes where people are taken to heaven or hell to begin a discussion about them.

Clearly explain that the most common idea is that people go to heaven or hell depending on how good they have been.

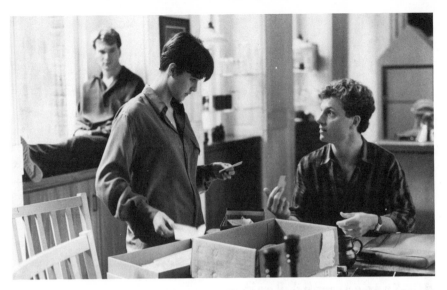

Sam Wheat (Patrick Swayze, left) is a ghost who watches Molly Jensen (Demi Moore, middle) and Carl Bruner (Tony Goldwyn, right) put away Sam's belongings following his death.

Share that the Bible teaches that no one is good enough to get into heaven. That is why Jesus died. Only those who have been covered by the blood of Jesus will enter heaven.

Make it clear that everyone is included: no one can escape death, and no one will get to heaven any other way. Each person has a choice to make.

Related Bible References

Romans 3:21–26 (righteousness from Christ); John 14:1–4, 1 Peter 1:3–4 (certainty of heaven); John 14:6 (Jesus as way to heaven); 2 Peter 2:4 (reality of hell).

Other Ideas

Ghost can also introduce a talk on sin. The movie portrays sin simply as action that is lacking love. If something is done in love (e.g. Sam living with his girlfriend), then it is not sin. The Bible describes and explains sin much differently. It would also be appropriate to use *Ghost* in a discussion of Satan, demons, and angels.

Jared Reed

28
Harvey

- Unrated
- 104 minutes
- A 1950 adaptation of the Mary Chase play of the same name

Synopsis and Review

In this classic film, Jimmy Stewart plays Elwood P. Dowd, a friendly, but eccentric man whose best friend and constant companion is a six-foot-tall invisible rabbit named Harvey.

Veta Louise Simmons (Josephine Hull) and her daughter Myrtle Mae (Victoria Horne), Dowd's sister and niece respectively, are deeply embarrassed by Dowd's oddball behavior and at last decide to commit him to a sanitarium, Chumley's Rest, run by Dr. Chumley (Cecil Kellaway).

In a hilarious and thought-provoking chain of events:

Dr. Lyman Sanderson (Charles Drake), the eager young psychiatrist at Chumley's, erroneously commits Veta Louise to the sanitarium!

A humiliated and angry Veta Louise orders her attorney, Judge Gaffney (William Lynn) to sue Chumley;

Chumley fires Dr. Sanderson;

The romantic relationship between Sanderson and Nurse Kelly (Peggy Dow) sours;

Myrtle Mae falls in love with Marvin Wilson (Jesse White), an orderly at Chumley's;

Everyone searches frantically for Dowd;

Dr. Chumley himself "meets" Harvey and becomes a kinder and gentler person.

In the end, Chumley rehires Dr. Sanderson; Sanderson and Kelly reconcile; and Dowd pleasantly agrees, at his aunt's request, to be injected with a formula (977) that will "restore his sanity." However, on hearing about the drastic personality changes the drug causes (easy-going, congenial recipients become tense, irritable people), Veta Louise changes her mind. Everyone is happy, and Dowd and Harvey walk off into the sunrise.

Suggestions for Viewing

This quirky and humorous film is worth watching in its entirety, but the final fifteen to twenty minutes contain the dialogue most worth discussing.

The only potential problem with the movie is that Dowd and his invisible rabbit friend, clearly the most attractive characters in this film, frequent bars and spend much of their time socializing over drinks. Hence, *Harvey* paints a disturbing and unrealistic picture of alcohol use and/or abuse.

Important Scenes and/or Quotes

1. Early in the film, Dowd makes two interesting comments: When the mailman says, "It's a beautiful day!" Dowd replies, "Every day's a beautiful day!"

   Later Dowd confesses, "I wrestled with reality for over twenty-five years and I'm happy to say I finally won out over it."

2. Discussing Harvey's ability and willingness to stop the clock so that one might go wherever he or she would rather be, Dowd tells Chumley: "So far I've never been able to think of any place I'd rather be. I always have a wonderful time just where I am, whomever I'm with. I'm having a fine time right now with you, Doctor."

3. Toward the end of the movie, Nurse Kelly and Dr. Sanderson find Dowd at Charlie's bar. Following him into the alley, they ask him exactly what he does. He answers:

   Well, Harvey and I sit in the bars and have a drink or two, play the jukebox, and soon the faces of all the other people, they turn toward mine and they smile. And they're saying, "We don't know your name, mister, but you're a very nice fellow."

Harvey and I warm ourselves in all these golden moments. We've entered as strangers, and soon we have friends. And they come over and they sit with us, and they drink with us, and they talk to us, and they tell about the big, terrible things they've done and the big, wonderful things they'll do . . . their hopes and their regrets, their loves and their hates—all very large because nobody ever brings anything small into a bar.

And then I introduce them to Harvey, and he's bigger and greater than anything they offer me. And when they leave, they leave impressed.

Discussion Questions

Was Harvey real? Why or why not?

In what ways does the Christian faith seem "crazy" to unbelievers?

Elwood P. Dowd is a genuinely nice person. He takes a sincere interest in everyone he meets. Why are so few people (including Christians) this kind and thoughtful?

Elwood P. Dowd seems to fully enjoy every moment of every day. What is the key to such a contented attitude?

What is it about Elwood P. Dowd that causes people to open up and say what they really think and feel? Why aren't people this way around most Christians? Why are people more likely to be honest in a bar than they are in a church?

Are you as eager to introduce others to Christ as Elwood P. Dowd is to introduce people to Harvey? If not, why not? In what ways is Harvey like Christ? Unlike Christ?

Outline of Talk or Wrap-up
Of Rabbits and Resurrections

1. Like Harvey, Christ is invisible (at least for now).
2. Like Harvey, Christ is real only to some people in the world.
3. Like Harvey, Christ is kind and accepting.
4. Like Harvey, Christ changes those he befriends.
5. Like Dowd, Christians ought to introduce others to their invisible friend.

Related Bible References

Use Paul's joyful attitude while in prison (Philippians) or his words to Timothy (1 Tim. 6:6–8) to discuss the possibility and necessity of contentment. Philippians 3:7–11 talks about the wonder of knowing Christ. Acts 4:1–20 tells the story of the arrest of Peter and John for preaching enthusiastically about the risen Christ. (Others might have doubted, but they had seen Christ with their own eyes and were excited about him! There was no stopping them.)

Other Ideas

Use *Harvey* before or during Holy Week (Palm Sunday through Resurrection Sunday) to capitalize on all the focus on the Easter Bunny.

Len Woods

29
Home Alone

- PG
- 105 minutes
- A 1990 film

Synopsis and Review

This 1990 Christmas blockbuster surprised the critics with tremendous ticket sales. It is a great comedy with a good message. Even though it has a Christmas setting, the movie certainly has year-round appeal.

Home Alone takes place in Chicago, in a well-to-do neighborhood where everyone leaves town for Christmas vacation, including the McAlisters who are going to France. The main character, Kevin McAlister, is the youngest in the family and always feels "dumped on." The night before his family's big trip, there is a big blowup in the kitchen for which Kevin is blamed. That night, Kevin wishes his family would disappear. The next morning, the family leaves in a tremendous hurry and, in the chaos, they leave Kevin at home, alone. When Kevin awakes and realizes that he is alone, he is convinced that he has wished his family into oblivion.

There is tremendous comedy as the eight-year-old enjoys life alone over the next few days. A classic Three Stooges type of episode occurs late in the show as two bumbling burglars attempt to rob Kevin's home. Kevin's defense system is guaranteed to bring laughter.

Suggestions for Viewing

This movie would be great to watch in its entirety. However, if most of the students have seen it a number of times, you may consider showing only selected scenes followed by discussion. There are two excellent topics addressed here separately—fear and family relationships. Combine these with the fine comedy and you will have a great meeting.

The PG rating is due to a few isolated swear words, outright parental defiance (which is later resolved), and some of the violent actions against the would-be burglars.

Important Scenes and Discussion Questions
Topic—Fear

Scene 1—Start with the kitchen scene when Kevin loses his cool and attacks his older brother. Let it run through the morning episode when Kevin is left behind. It's great fun to see him realize that he is alone. We get an introduction to Kevin's fear of the furnace in the basement. Stop before Kevin reaches his brother's trunk.

Discussion Questions:

What were some fears you had when you were about Kevin's age?

How did you deal with your fears?

Whom did you tell about your fears?

How would Kevin's siblings have responded to his fear?

Scene 2—Explain that Buzz, Kevin's older brother, has told Kevin that the elderly man who lives next door is a shovel murderer. Then show the burglars casing the street in their van; stop after Kevin sees the old man and runs screaming into the house.

Discussion Questions:

What were some of the scary stories that used to circulate around your neighborhood or school when you were younger?

Tell about any strange characters in your neighborhood or community that people were afraid of.

You may have felt that you had once conquered a fear, only to discover later that you had not. Tell us about it.

Scene 3—Explain that in the next scene Kevin conquers his fear of the furnace. Ask the group to watch how he does this. Run the tape through the time when the burglar runs away from the "shooting" he hears inside the house. (This is a short scene.)

Discussion Questions:

How did Kevin conquer his fear of the furnace?

In what other ways do people conquer their fears?

Scene 4—This may be the most memorable episode in *Home Alone*. It is the church scene where Kevin actually meets the old man. Both of them are very helpful to each other. Ask half the group to watch for the counsel on fear given by the old man and the other half to watch for counsel given by Kevin.

Discussion Questions:

Review what the two groups heard (e.g. a person is never too old to be afraid, fear is often fear of the unknown, etc.)

What kind of fears might an older person have?

Scene 5—Fast forward to the funniest part of the movie, Kevin's battle with the burglars. Begin when he sits down to eat, and end as Kevin waves to the criminals riding off in the patrol car.

Discussion Questions:

Who ultimately rescued Kevin?

It's interesting that the person Kevin feared actually became a great help to him. When has that happened to you?

Scene 6—Show the final and most heartwarming scene of the film. Begin when the truck drives up with Kevin's mom. This includes the family's return and the reunification of the old man's family. Run to the end.

Discussion Questions:

The old man's fear of rejection had kept him from talking to his son. Tell about a time you hesitated to talk to someone for fear of their response.

Outline of Talk or Wrap-up
On Fear

Explain that fear of the unknown is paralyzing. Most of our concerns, however, are unfounded. Emphasize that fear will be part of our experience throughout our lives. We must develop good habits of dealing with fear. Point out practical ways to deal with fear—facing up to our fears; recognizing the irrationality of fear; talking to someone about our fears; turning to God.

Related Bible References

2 Timothy 1:6–7 (God is not a God of fear); Psalm 27 (a great Psalm about many fears); Psalm 55:22 (give God your fears).

Important Scenes and Discussion Questions
Topic—Family Relationships

Scene 1—Run the opening scene with the police officer, the pizza delivery boy, and the kitchen episode. Stop the tape when the storm begins at night. (About fifteen minutes long.)
Discussion Questions:

Tell about a time when you, like Kevin, said: "When I grow up, I'm going to live alone!"

Share about a time when you felt everyone in the family was "dumpin' on you."

Kevin wished that his whole family would disappear. What's a wish you would have for your family?

Scene 2—Continue with the morning episode when Kevin is unwittingly left behind. It's great fun to see him realize he is alone. Stop before Kevin opens his brother's trunk.
Discussion Questions:

How would life be better without your family?

What things would be more enjoyable? Whom would you miss the most? the least?

Scene 3—Move to the family waiting in the apartment in Paris. Enjoy the pizza delivery scene. You begin to see real love and concern in Kevin's mom's attempts to get home. Stop after Kevin talks to the family picture and begins to regret his wish.

Discussion Questions:

Who in your family would react like Buzz?

Who would be most likely to say the kinds of things Kevin's sister said?

If you had a picture of your family in front of you, what kinds of feelings would you have as you studied it?

Scene 4—Show the time when Kevin goes to Santa to ask for his family's return. Continue through the church scene. Before running this scene, ask half the group to watch for Kevin's true feelings about his family. The other half should look for the old man's feelings for his family.

Discussion Questions:

Ask for the observations of the two groups.

What kind of "family" advice do we hear from the characters?

Scene 5—Fast forward to the funniest part of the movie, Kevin's battle with the burglars. Begin when Kevin sits down to eat, and end as he waves to the criminals riding off in the patrol car. Just enjoy the slapstick humor.

Scene 6—Show the final and most heartwarming scene of the film. Begin when the truck drives up with Kevin's mom. This includes the family's return and the reunification of the old man's family. Run to the end.

Discussion Questions:

What did Kevin's mother say to him?

What do you think the old man said to his son?

Why is it so hard to say we are sorry? Tell about a time you had to apologize.

Outline of Talk or Wrap-up
On Family

Point out that it is a common experience to feel as though you're being "dumped on" in a family. Our family members often make mistakes, and we need to allow them the freedom to fail. Usually it's a misperception on our part.

Most importantly, we need to be able to say we are sorry and to accept apologies.

Sometimes God allows difficult situations to arise in our families to remind us how much we really do care for each other.

Related Bible References

Exodus 20:12 (honor your parents); Ephesians 6:1–3.

Gary Schulte

30

It Happened One Night

- Unrated
- 105 minutes
- A 1934 film

Synopsis and Review

This classic romantic comedy won the Academy Award in 1934 for Best Picture. Clark Gable, Claudette Colbert, Frank Capra, and Robert Riskin also won for Best Actor, Best Actress, Best Director, and Best Screenplay respectively.

Colbert plays Ellie Andrews, a spoiled rich girl who has just wed a young aviator, King Westley (Jameson Thomas). Her father, Wall Street tycoon Alexander Andrews (Walter Connolly), opposes the union, believing the man to be a fortune hunter. Andrews orders his private detectives to "kidnap" his daughter and spirit her away to the family yacht, anchored off the coast of Miami, where he hopes he can talk her out of her foolish decision and have the marriage annulled.

The plan is a disaster. The father's and daughter's strong-willed personalities clash, and Ellie dives overboard. After swimming safely to shore, she purchases a bus ticket to New York, hoping to elude her father's henchmen and be reunited with Westley.

With a $10,000 reward being offered for her safe return, Ellie Andrews' whereabouts are front-page news.

On her journey north, Ellie meets Gable's character, Peter Warne, a recently-fired newspaper reporter. On learning Miss Andrews' identity, Warne figures he will have the scoop of a lifetime if he can accompany her to New York and write daily news reports about her "against-all-odds" effort to be reunited with Westley.

Sparks fly and love ultimately blooms in this reverse Cinderella tale. The poor reporter wins the affection of the rich girl, and several classic moments take place along the way.

Suggestions for Viewing

As one of Hollywood's most honored movies, featuring two of its all-time greatest stars, *It Happened One Night* should be viewed by everyone. It is romantic comedy at its finest.

However, if time is short you can show any of the following selected scenes:

1. When Peter and Ellie miss the bus at one of its first stops and he identifies her as the missing heiress. She offers to buy him off if he doesn't reveal her whereabouts. He lectures her for being so snooty. The dialogue is snappy and the chemistry between the two stars is perfect.
2. When Peter and Ellie try their hand at hitchhiking.
3. When Peter and Ellie stay in an auto camp cabin together for the second time (sleeping apart, separated by Peter's clothesline and blanket, or as he calls the divider, the "Walls of Jericho"). Ellie declares her love for Peter. It is a touching scene.

   This scene is also pivotal, for Peter decides to ask Ellie to marry him. But he needs money. Leaving in the middle of the night, he returns to New York to write the big news story that will pay him one thousand dollars. His plan is to get the money and return before morning; however, Ellie awakes to find him gone. Thinking she has been spurned, she calls her father and goes back to Westley.

   At this point, Peter thinks *he* has been jilted! It is a classic case of misunderstanding.

It Happened One Night is a film classic for the whole family. The only disturbing aspect is the movie's rather cavalier attitude toward the marriage of Ellie and Westley. Specifically, Ellie *is* already married to Westley. Her "kidnapping" apparently takes place before the marriage is consummated. Mr. Andrews insists on having the marriage annulled. But she, in arguing with her father about her union with Westley, remarks:

Look. Why can't we give it a trial: let's say . . . for a year or so.
If it's wrong, King and I will be the first to know it. We can get a
divorce, can't we?

Important Scenes and/or Quotes

When an angry and hurt Peter visits Ellie's father to be reim-
bursed for his expenses (under the assumption that he's been
dumped), the following dialogue takes place.

Andrews:	And this is what you want—thirty-nine dollars and sixty cents?
Peter:	Why not? I'm not charging you for the time I wasted.
Andrews:	Yes, I know . . . but . . .
Peter:	What's the matter? Isn't it cheap enough? A trip like that would cost *you* a thousand dollars! Maybe more!
Andrews:	Let me get this straight. You want this thirty-nine sixty in addition to the ten thousand dollars?
Peter:	What ten thousand?
Andrews:	The reward.
Peter:	(sharply) Who said anything about a reward!
Andrews:	(smiling) I'm afraid I'm a little confused. You see, I assumed you were coming here for . . .
Peter:	(impatiently) All I want is thirty-nine sixty. If you'll give me a check, I'll get out of this place. It gives me the jitters.
Andrews:	You're a peculiar chap.
Peter:	(irritably) We'll go into that some other time.
Andrews:	The average man would go after the reward. All you seem to . . .
Peter:	Listen, did anybody ever make a sucker of you? This is a matter of principle. Something you probably wouldn't understand. (He burns at the thought.) When somebody takes me for a buggy ride I don't like the idea of having to pay for the privilege.
Andrews:	You were taken for a buggy ride?
Peter:	Yeah . . . with all the trimmings. Now, how about the check. Do I get it?
Andrews:	(smiling) Certainly. Here you are. Do you mind if I ask you something frankly. Do you love my daughter?
Peter:	(evasively, while folding the check) A guy that'd fall in love with your daughter should have his head examined.
Andrews:	That's an evasion.

| Peter: | She grabbed herself a perfect running mate. King Westley! The pill of the century! What she needs is a guy that'd *take a sock at her every day, whether it's coming to her or not.* |

(A close view of the two shows Andrews smiling: here is the perfect man for his headstrong daughter.)

Peter:	If you had half the brains you're supposed to have, you'd have done it yourself . . . long ago.
Andrews:	Do you love her?
Peter:	A normal human being couldn't live under the same roof with her, without going nuts. She's my idea of nothing!
Andrews:	I asked you a question. Do you love her?
Peter:	(snapping it out) Yes! but don't hold that against me. I'm a little screwy myself.

Discussion Questions

How can people from different socio-economic backgrounds be happy together?

Ellie and Peter wait until they marry to have sex. How would the movie be different if it were filmed today?

Ellie and King Westley must have already been wed since Ellie's father spoke of having their marriage annulled. (Though the movie suggests that they had not yet consummated their relationship through sex.) How do you suppose God views annulment?

Ellie and Peter "fall in love" during their journey north. Is love primarily a feeling, or is it a commitment revealed by acts of kindness? What acts of kindness do Ellie and Peter show for each other?

Outline of Talk or Wrap-up
Hollywood Romance vs. Loving by the Book

1. Love is a commitment, not a crazy feeling that comes over you or something you fall into and out of.
2. Love is not always exotic and romantic.
3. Love does not equal sex.
4. Love (married love) is for life.

Related Bible References

1 Corinthians 13 is the classic "love chapter" of the Bible. (You might choose to compare this with the love demonstrated in the movie.) Matthew 19 indicates the seriousness and permanence with which God views marriage vows. 1 Thessalonians 4:3–8 shows God's requirements for sexual purity.

Other Ideas

Show *It Happened One Night* at a social just before Valentine's Day. Then discuss it at your next meeting.

Len Woods

31

It's a Wonderful Life

- Unrated
- 129 minutes
- A 1946 film

Synopsis and Review

Jimmy Stewart stars in this holiday classic about a despondent businessman who is given a supernatural glimpse of how wonderful his life really is.

George Bailey (Stewart) is an honest, likable man who has suffered a lifetime of personal disappointments. Despite his dreams ("I'm shaking the dust of this crummy little town off my feet and I'm going to see the world!"), George has never been able to get out of sleepy little Bedford Falls. Despite big career plans to "do something big and important" like "design new buildings" and "plan modern cities," George has been forced to manage his family's "cheap, penny-ante Building and Loan." While a classmate, Sam Wainwright (Frank Albertson), makes a fortune in manufacturing, and a brother, Harry Bailey (Todd Karns), finds fame as a college football star and later as a war hero, George sees his life as one colossal failure. A business crisis on Christmas Eve (a misplaced $8,000 bank deposit) is the last straw. George decides to take his own life.

Enter Clarence (Henry Travers), George's guardian angel, who foils the suicide attempt and grants George's wish "that I'd never been born."

A nightmarish vision of what the world would have been like without him causes George to rethink the powerful and positive influence he's had on so many others. With a newfound joy for life, George runs home to find himself showered with love and support from all his friends

129

and neighbors. George realizes that "no man is a failure who has friends."

Suggestions for Viewing

It's a Wonderful Life is such a wonderful story that you'll probably want to watch the entire film. Perhaps your group could watch the movie in the context of a social event (i.e. a Christmas party) and then discuss it at the next youth meeting or Bible study time.

Another reason this movie should be viewed in its entirety is that it depends heavily on flashbacks. Certain references and/or scenes do not stand alone.

A good discussion can be generated, however, by simply sharing the plot line and then by having the group watch the final twenty to twenty-five minutes of the film. Begin with the scene where George Bailey goes to see Herbert Potter (Lionel Barrymore), his business rival and the town "Scrooge," to ask for help. Everything in the film up to this point is actually background material. The story really begins here, for on leaving Potter's office, George contemplates suicide, meets Clarence, and has his wish ("that I'd never been born") granted.

Find this pivotal moment in *It's a Wonderful Life* immediately after scenes in which:

George's bumbling Uncle Billy (Thomas Mitchell) misplaces the $8,000 deposit.

George and Uncle Billy search frantically and futilely for the money.

George comes home and takes out his frustration on his family.

Important Scenes and/or Quotes

1. George runs frantically about in his dream trying to make sense of a world which is darker and uglier because he wasn't alive to make a difference. At last Clarence remarks:

   Strange, isn't it? Each man's life touches so many other lives, and when he isn't around he leaves an awful hole, doesn't he?

2. Moments later, George cries out in despair:

Clarence! Clarence! Help me, Clarence. Get me back. Get me back. I don't care what happens to me. Only get me back to my wife and kids. Help me, Clarence, please. Please! I want to live again! I want to live again. I want to live again. Please, God, let me live again.

Discussion Questions

When hard times hit, why do we so easily forget all the good things in our lives?

Put yourself in George Bailey's place. How would you have handled similar disappointments or trials in life?

What unrealized dreams or goals would cause you to look back on your life as a failure?

Comment on the note Clarence inscribed for George Bailey in the book *Tom Sawyer*. Is it really true that "no man is a failure who has friends"? Why or why not?

Harry Bailey called his brother George "the richest man in town." What did Harry mean?

How would the world be different if you had never been born?

Outline of Talk or Wrap-up

Talks and/or discussions could pursue any one of several themes.

Option #1:

Use the powerful message of *It's a Wonderful Life* to discuss the theme of **satisfaction.**

    A. Most people look for satisfaction in personal achievement (George Bailey), in wealth (Sam Wainwright), or in fame (Harry Bailey).

    B. *Real* satisfaction is found in a relationship with God and friendships with others.

Option #2:

Use the movie to illustrate that true **contentment** doesn't depend on circumstances.

    A. Life seldom works out as we think it will.

    B. Hard times often bombard us.

    C. Despite disappointments and discouragement, we can still find contentment by relying on God and remembering his blessings (especially our friendships).

Option #3:

Emphasize **faithfulness**.

    A. While it is good to have goals and dreams in life (as George Bailey did) we must be willing to do whatever God wants and go where he leads. God's plan is always perfect, though we may not be able to see the wisdom at the time.

    B. When God shuts one door, he opens another that leads to deeper satisfaction.

    C. What counts most with God is not doing something dramatic, but being faithful in the everyday situations of life.

        1. Our desire to make a difference.

        2. God's desire that we be faithful.

        3. The difference we make by being faithful.

Related Bible References

The story of Joseph (Gen. 39–50) is an excellent parallel to the dilemma faced by George Bailey. Joseph is wrongly accused. He gets a "raw deal" from life; and yet, because he trusts in God's purpose and plan, he ultimately is vindicated and blessed. Faithful servants of God will encounter hard times, yet they are always rewarded in the end. Ecclesiastes demonstrates the truth that accomplishments, wealth, and fame do not result in happiness. Only a relationship with God and enjoyment of his blessings (including friendships) can bring satisfaction. Philippians 4:10–19 is a great passage on contentment.

Other Ideas

It's a Wonderful Life can also be used to launch discussions about friendship, suicide, or even angels.

Len Woods

32

The Journey of Natty Gann

- PG
- 101 minutes
- A 1985 film

Synopsis and Review

This Depression-era film chronicles the cross-country journey of a young girl, Natty Gann (Meredith Salenger). With her mother dead and her father, Sol (Ray Wise), working in a Washington logging camp, Natty is left in the care of an acquaintance of her father's in Chicago, a woman named Connie (Lainie Kazan).

When tension arises between Natty and Connie, the girl sets out in search of her father. Her cross-country trek leads her through a variety of adventures. She is joined at times by a loyal wolf and an older teenage boy named Harry (John Cusack).

Natty's father is told she is dead after her wallet is found beneath a train wreck in Colorado. Their eventual reunion is satisfying for characters and viewers alike.

Natty Gann shows a young teen's grit and endurance to stand up for what she believes and to live her life completely for one purpose—being reunited with her father.

Suggestions for Viewing

This is not a movie of poignant moments. Rather, it is in watching the whole that viewers understand Natty's strong will and perseverance. So watch *Natty Gann* from beginning to end if possible.

It seems Hollywood is unable to put out a family movie without some swearing. However, the profanity in this film is neither excessive nor unbelievable, given the setting.

Discussion Questions

What would give Natty the perseverance to go on in the face of so much opposition?

What values do you think were important to Natty?

What are your top two values in life?

What does this film tell us about Natty's relationship with her father? How important is your family to you? What do you do to show your family members how you feel about them?

What if you had to go through lots of trials and hardship to stay true to your relationship with Jesus Christ? Would you be willing? At what point do you think you'd break down? What if defending your faith meant death?

What did God go through to reach us when we were far away from him? How should that affect the way we live today?

What one thing could you do to stand up for Christ in your daily life?

Outline of Talk or Wrap-up

Spend five or ten minutes explaining to students how God continually seeks us, how he desires a relationship with us so much that he will go to any length to ensure that—even continually forgiving us when we sin against him.

Continue the perseverance train of thought, but switch to our response to God. Explain the need for endurance in defending God. The Bible calls us his ambassadors (2 Cor. 5:20). We carry a great responsibility in the visual expressions of Christ's love and compassion, as well as God's justice. Though Jesus tells us his yoke is easy, it's still a yoke! There are fields to be plowed, and we're the oxen. Wrap up by asking the students to write down some kind of tangible action they will take (in response to the last discussion question) for Christ.

Related Bible References

Job 23:10; Ecclesiastes 9:10; Matthew 24:13; 2 Timothy 2:1–3; Judges 8:4.

Other Ideas

Tie in this lesson with some type of stressful activity—a long bike trip, a wilderness hike, or a workday. Draw parallels from experience and the need to press on and "go for it."

Mark Oestreicher

33
The Karate Kid

- PG
- 126 minutes
- A 1984 film

Synopsis and Review

The Karate Kid is a heartwarming story about friendship and mentor relationships. Daniel (Ralph Macchio) is a Newark, New Jersey teenager who moves with his mother, Lucille (Randee Heller), to Los Angeles. There he becomes friends with an older Japanese man, Miyagi (Noriyuki "Pat" Morita), who is the maintenance man for their apartment building.

Daniel finds the adjustment to his new school unusually rough when he begins to date the girlfriend of the toughest boy in the senior class. This boy and his friends are being trained by a ruthless karate instructor who encourages violence and intimidation. They practice their karate and intimidation on Daniel until a fateful night when Miyagi emerges out of the shadows to rescue Daniel with a display of his skill as a karate master. Miyagi decides to protect Daniel more permanently by taking him on as a private student.

The movie portrays the development of a mentor/friend relationship as Miyagi leads Daniel through some unusual training techniques: waxing cars, painting fences, and sanding decks. Daniel complains that he is not learning karate, but Miyagi knows his training system.

The final sequence of the movie is a rousing, climactic fight scene where Daniel faces the boys who had beaten him and their ruthless instructor in a karate tournament. Daniel overcomes injury and unethical tactics to win the trophy, the girl, and a lasting relationship with his mentor, Miyagi.

Suggestions for Viewing

The best scenes to use as discussion starters are the training scenes (approximately halfway into the movie, just after Daniel and his girlfriend visit the amusement park) and the final fight scene (the last twelve minutes of the movie).

Important Scenes and/or Quotes

Show the training scene following the trip to the amusement park. Daniel rides his bike into Miyagi's compound. A series of brief episodes leads to an angry confrontation between Daniel and Miyagi.

Daniel sands the wooden deck (three minutes).

Miyagi catches the fly with chopsticks (one minute thirty seconds).

Daniel paints the fence (three minutes). When Daniel thinks he is finished, Miyagi asks "Both sides?"

Daniel paints the house and erupts into an angry confrontation with Miyagi because he is just free labor and is not learning karate (four minutes twenty seconds). (Caution: there are four curses in Daniel's outburst.) The result of the outburst is a powerful scene where Miyagi shows Daniel how all the tasks he has been doing are preparing his muscles for the basic moves of karate.

Daniel and Miyagi go to the beach to practice balance (three minutes ten seconds). Daniel sees Miyagi practicing the crane move which he will ultimately learn and use to win the tournament. He also watches Miyagi deal with ridicule and harassment by keeping his strength and skill under control.

Discussion Questions

Why was Daniel so upset with Miyagi? What was Miyagi doing for Daniel that he didn't realize? What do you imagine Daniel was thinking as he went home that night?

What similarities are there between how Miyagi taught Daniel the basics of karate and how someone teaches us to be a follower of Jesus Christ? How might we resist or misunderstand the spiritual training we need?

What difficult or challenging experiences (that you possibly disliked at the time) have strengthened your relationship with Jesus Christ and prepared you for the spiritual battles you face?

What are some of the basic "moves" we must learn to be effective Christians?

When Daniel told Miyagi he wanted to learn the crane move, Miyagi told him he needed to learn to stand before he could run. How do young Christians try to rush into deep spiritual matters before mastering the basics?

Outline of Talk or Wrap-up

1. Our faith in Jesus is just the beginning of a life-long relationship with him.

2. Our goal is to become like Jesus. God is interested in developing our character (who we are) to reflect Jesus.

3. God often uses ordinary circumstances to teach us important, basic lessons about our relationship with him. We learn how to obey God by obeying our parents. We learn how to love selflessly and sacrificially by how we treat our family members. We learn the value of truth and integrity by how we speak and act on our jobs. There are many examples.

4. God uses prayer, daily Bible reading, and church involvement to strengthen us spiritually for the major battle we will face some time in the future. We must be strong in the basics of the faith so God can use us in some special way at a crucial moment in the future.

5. We must keep our eyes on the goal of becoming like Christ and be obedient to God's training plan for us each day. Then we will be ready to fight for God and see him win a great victory through us—perhaps in our family, our school, or with our friends.

This is a good time to watch the final fight scene of the movie. You can introduce it by talking about the ultimate victory which Christ has won over evil and how he can use us each day to fight for him in an evil world. This is a great way to close.

Related Bible References

1 Corinthians 9:24–27; Philippians 3:12–14; 1 Timothy 4:12–16; 2 Timothy 2:3–7; 2 Timothy 4:7–8; Hebrews 12:1, 2, 5–12.

Jack Crabtree

34
The Karate Kid Part 2

- PG
- 113 minutes
- A 1986 film

Synopsis and Review

The Karate Kid Part 2 is the sequel of the surprise hit *The Karate Kid*. Daniel Larusso (Ralph Macchio), fresh off his victory in the All Valley Karate Tournament, continues his relationship with his mentor, Miyagi (Pat Morita). Together they learn about some of the bigger battles of life as they travel to Okinawa, Japan to confront Miyagi's archenemy from long ago, Sato (Danny Kamekona), and his nasty nephew, Chozen (Yuzi Okumoto).

For the most part this is a forgettable movie—a typical sequel. The first ten minutes provide a reprise of the first movie and add a post-victory scene which is worth discussing.

Suggestions for Viewing

Show the first ten minutes of the movie where the original *Karate Kid* story is summarized culminating with the famous crane kick that Daniel uses to defeat his unethical opponents. The sequel picks up immediately after that winning moment. As Daniel and Miyagi exit the arena they see the karate master of the defeated team abusing the young man who lost the match. Miyagi confronts the win-at-all-costs coach and demonstrates his strength and mercy. Stop the video after Daniel and Miyagi drive away from the scene.

Important Scenes and/or Quotes

When Miyagi confronts the evil karate master, he is the model of strength and confidence under control, demanding justice and fair play with firmness and confidence. He coolly evades the attacks of his enemy and positions himself to strike a lethal blow. Then, with the villain kneeling helpless before him, Miyagi repeats the code this evil teacher has taught to his students. "Mercy is for the weak. When man face you, he is enemy. Enemy deserves no mercy." Raising his hand and shouting, Miyagi stops short of striking the blow and tweaks his nose instead. As they walk away, Daniel asks: "You could have killed him. Why didn't you?" Miyagi answers, "For person with no forgiveness in heart, living even worse punishment than death."

Discussion Questions

Explain why you think Miyagi was right or wrong in how he handled the evil karate master.

What are some of Miyagi's characteristics that impress you?

Explain Miyagi's statement about no forgiveness being a worse punishment than death.

Tell about a time when you (or someone you know) were consumed by anger and hatred toward a person who had hurt you in some way. If you had Miyagi's karate skill what would you have done to that person?

The Bible talks about loving our enemies and doing good to those who do evil to us. How would a person ever love his or her enemies?

Describe any experiences you have had when you either held on to anger and hatred for another person for a long time or when you forgave or showed mercy to someone who had hurt you deeply. What did either of those attitudes or actions do to you during that time?

How can a person become less vengeful and more forgiving?

Outline of Talk or Wrap-up

Say something like: "Jesus taught his disciples to break one of the most accepted rules of society. Instead of paying back evil for evil, we are to return good for evil.

"Listen to some of the most unbelievable statements Jesus ever made." Read Matthew 5:38–48.

"Jesus teaches us to love with a powerful love that can break the cycle of revenge and retribution. Contrary to popular opinion, anyone who turns the other cheek or goes the extra mile is not a wimp. People like that, in fact, are stronger, but they keep their strength under control and channel it toward constructive purposes.

"When Martin Luther King, Jr. and his followers were abused as they demonstrated for civil rights, they responded without returning violence. Their tactics changed the attitude of our whole nation and brought higher levels of civil rights and equality.

"Let's think of some practical ways we can practice this strong love Jesus commands." (Tell a story about a situation where you had to choose how to respond to some evil person or situation.)

"Jesus calls us to an even greater challenge than restraining our strength from an evil and destructive response. He calls us to show mercy and forgiveness to our enemies.

"The standard for the extent of our forgiveness is the forgiveness and mercy God has shown to us." Read Ephesians 4:32.

"Hatred and bitterness toward another person become a chain on our lives. Forgiveness and mercy give us freedom. Paul, the apostle, had many reasons to be bitter and angry. Instead he left those matters of judgment in God's hands and lived as a truly free man (even when he was in prison) because his spirit was focused on the love and mercy of God. No one could hurt him so deeply that he would forget God's promises.

"Do you want to be enslaved to anger and revenge? Would you rather be free? Whatever situation or person in your life is causing you to be full of anger and revenge, just picture yourself tweaking that person on the nose and walking away. Forgive them and move on."

Related Bible References

Romans 12:9–21; Colossians 3:13; 2 Corinthians 2:10; Luke 6:37; Matthew 6:10–15; Matthew 18:21–35.

Jack Crabtree

35
King David

- PG-13
- 114 minutes
- A 1985 film

Synopsis and Review

Richard Gere is King David in this elaborate piece recalling the life and times of the Hebrew king and psalmist. The costuming, location, and huge cast transport the viewer into the life of David. Insight is gained into the life of the man "after God's heart." But the "humanness" of David's sins is also (almost too clearly) presented. Several of David's psalms take on new life when overlaid on the many situations he faced. Some of the high points are the exciting battle with Goliath (Luigi Montefiori), David's faithful service to King Saul (Edward Woodward), and his continuous love for rebellious Prince Absalom (Jean-Marc Barr).

Suggestions for Viewing

This film certainly warrants the PG-13 rating with several graphic battles; the partial nudity of David's wedding night and the Bathsheba scenes also lead to the rating. However, the movie as a whole is exceptionally helpful in understanding the life, times, and psalms of David.

Important Scenes and Discussion Questions

Show the scene when young David arrives at the Philistine battlefield to comfort King Saul. Explain that God's Spirit has been removed from Saul, resulting in torment for which the only cure is David's soothing psalms on the harp. Let it run until the narration following Israel's routing of the Philistines.

> How were these experiences in David's life similar to or different from those you had envisioned when reading the Bible?
>
> What impressed you about these scenes?
>
> David was a man who "sought after God's own heart" (1 Sam. 13:14). What are other high points in his life? (spared Saul's life—1 Sam. 24:10–12; returned the Ark, dancing before God—2 Sam. 6:12–15; laid plans for building the temple—1 Chron. 22:5; wrote many great psalms including Pss. 23 and 51).

Absalom, David's heir to the throne, was banished from the kingdom due to his avenging his sister Tamar's rape (2 Sam. 13—14). This is part of God's punishment of David for his sin with Bathsheba. View the scene beginning where Absalom is leaving in exile. Through the prophet Nathan, God confronts David with his great sin (2 Sam. 12). It is a gripping moment. Pause the machine during the snow shower that follows David's repentant psalm.

> In what ways do these scenes give you new insight into the Psalms?
>
> David reacted in complete repentance. What are some ways he could have reacted instead? (blame someone else, justify his actions, denial)
>
> How was God's mercy shown toward David in the punishment?

Outline of Talk or Wrap-up

A model for repentance, David's prayer—Psalm 51

1. 1–2—David reminds himself of God's mercy; no sin is too great; David is afraid that what happened to Saul might happen to him (God may remove his Spirit from him).
2. 3–6—David acknowledges sin: "I broke rules; your rules!" He doesn't blame God for putting Bathsheba in sight.

3. 7–12—David asks for cleansing for the future. Hyssop was a tree from which they would take a branch, dip it in blood and sprinkle over someone to be healed of a disease. David wanted to be healed of the disease of sin.
4. 11—David pleads for God to not remove his Spirit from him as he had done to Saul.
5. 13–17—David wants to tell others of this forgiving God; David didn't want to punish himself any longer.

This psalm is a great model to follow for our own repentance.

Other Ideas

Sing the praise song "Create in Me a Clean Heart, O God." Having studied Psalm 51, the line "cast me not away from thy presence, oh Lord, and take not thy Holy Spirit from me" comes alive in a new way.

Gary Schulte

36
Kramer vs. Kramer

- PG
- 105 minutes
- A 1979 film

Synopsis and Review

Ted Kramer (Dustin Hoffman) is bright, driven, climbing the corporate ladder, and losing his wife. Joanna Kramer (Meryl Streep) can't cope any longer with her successful but disinterested and insensitive husband, so she leaves him and their young son Billy (Justin Henry) and goes off to find herself. Ted is about as well-prepared to be a single father as Saddam Hussein is to be the next Pope, so the adjustment is rough and overwhelming. Billy, understandably, is a confused, hurt, and frightened little boy trying to come to grips with life without Mommy. *Kramer vs. Kramer* is the story of how these three people deal with the destruction of their family.

Suggestions for Viewing

Having seen this film a few times already, I thought I could easily sit through it again and dissect it for the purposes of this review. Even though I had seen it—and even used it as the basis for a meeting with high schoolers—and in spite of the fact that it is now over ten years old, *Kramer vs. Kramer* has lost none of its impact. It is still the most powerful movie I have ever seen dealing with the impact divorce has on a family; and it deserves to be seen in its entirety. At one hour, forty-five minutes in length, it is possible to show the whole movie in a slightly longer than usual meeting format.

If you choose not to show it all, check the scenes described below.

Warning: there is some profanity, brief nudity, and a suggested sexual scene.

Important Scenes and/or Quotes

1. The first seven and one half minutes show Joanna leaving and set up the conflict that the rest of the movie will deal with.

2. Just after this, Ted and his neighbor Margaret (Jane Alexander) have an argument over Joanna's walking out. Defending her friend, Margaret declares that it took a lot of courage for Joanna to do what she did. Ted asks, "How much courage does it take to walk out on your kid?"

3. At approximately thirty-five minutes, there is a poignant scene with Ted and Billy at the dinner table. Both touching and funny, it will probably hit home with most kids of divorce (and others, too). The payoff line in this section (which lasts till about the forty-two minute mark) comes when Billy asks his father, "That's why Mommy left, isn't it? 'Cause I was bad?" This will score a direct hit with every child of divorce.

4. At one hour and twelve minutes, the courtroom scene begins. It lasts for approximately twenty minutes, but may be worth showing in its entirety. Some highlights:

Ted's attorney cross-examines Joanna, asking her if Ted was abusive, an alcoholic, unfaithful, or a poor provider. When she answers "No," he replies, "I can certainly see why you left him."

There is a touching scene with Ted on the stand, asking rhetorically, "What makes a parent a good parent?" After admitting that he is far from perfect, he adds, "But I'm *there*." Ted's evolution as a parent is dramatic.

5. Probably the most moving sequence is the final "French toast" scene. The contrast with the first time Ted and Billy tried to get through breakfast on their own is stark.

6. The final scene—Joanna's "reversal"—is riveting and surprising. It will be interesting to see how various kids respond to what she does, positively or negatively.

Discussion Questions

You may as well deal with the obvious first. Ask how many in your group have been through their parents' divorce. How many have been through more than one?

What were Joanna's reasons for leaving? How much of the blame for what happened should Ted share?

What do you think of Ted's remark, "How much courage does it take to walk out on your kid?"

Billy's assumption that his mommy left because *he* was bad is almost universal among kids of divorce. Explore how many of your kids have felt or still feel that way.

How do you feel about the judge awarding custody to Joanna? Why do you think mothers almost always win custody battles?

Why do so many marriages end in divorce?

What do you think about what Joanna did at the end? Was it admirable, or do you think it simply meant she put all of them through the misery of a court battle for nothing?

If you were Billy, whom would you want to live with? Why?

Outline of Talk or Wrap-up

Kramer vs. Kramer is loaded with so much heavy stuff that you can use it to launch a number of discussions. I suggest you zero in on one of the following:

1. Many in our society view marriage as just another civil contract, to be entered into and gotten out of on the whim of the participants. Contrast this with the Bible's view of marriage as God's own sacred institution, a covenant between a man and a woman before God Almighty. (see Gen. 2:18–25; Matt. 19:3–12; 1 Cor. 7; Eph. 5:22–33; Col. 3:18–21.)

2. Divorce is one of the most traumatic events that can take place in the life of a child. Most children of divorce

will admit that it causes them great pain and insecurity. Perhaps most troubling of all is the fact that so many children (regardless of their ages) do in fact blame themselves for their parents' divorce. It may be one of the most significant ways you can minister to your young people to tell them that their parents' divorce was not their fault, even if one or both parents told them it was. You may be able to help them be free from an enormous load of false (and debilitating) guilt.

Related Bible References

See above.

Other Ideas

Bring in one or more of the following to be your guest speaker/panel: a counselor or therapist who specializes in dealing with families touched by divorce; an adult man and woman who have been divorced (but not from each other!); someone whose parents divorced who has worked through a lot of his/her pain and conflict as a result. Be sure you know where you want the discussion to go so you don't get any surprises.

Kent Keller

37

Les Miserables

- Unrated
- 178 minutes
- A 1978 film based on the book by Victor Hugo

Synopsis and Review

Les Miserables is a study on forgiveness centering around the lives of two very different men. Jean Valjean (Richard Jordan) is a woodcutter who, in order to feed his family, breaks into a bakery. He is caught and sent to jail. After nineteen years in prison, he escapes. As an escaped convict, he survives by stealing.

Late one evening he knocks on the door of a priest in an unfamiliar town, hoping to find food and shelter. The maid shoos him away, but the priest invites him in, treating him as an honored guest.

That night as everyone else sleeps, Jean steals most of the silver in the house and slips away. After being captured by the police, he insists that the silver was a gift from the priest. Not believing him, the police escort him back to the home of the priest. As Jean stands facing the man whom he has just robbed, the priest explains to the officers that all of the silver was truly a gift, but that Jean forgot two items, silver candle holders. The priest gives them to Jean but demands that Jean now live as an honest man since his life has been bought by the priest.

Jean's life is changed. At last, someone believes in him. He has been forgiven by the priest. Now, he can forgive the world for mistreating him and begin to help others who might be in trouble.

Jean's life is spent helping others, especially the daughter of a dying woman for whom he promised to care. He raises her as his daughter.

Javert (Anthony Perkins), the other main character, is a police officer. Having grown up the son of a prisoner, hate has filled his heart. With others and with himself, he demands total justice, leaving no space for mercy. Though these two men initially meet while Jean is a prisoner and Javert is a guard, their lives intertwine as Javert dedicates his life to bringing Jean to justice.

Their paths cross many times but Jean always seems to elude his captor. But when Javert is condemned to die as a spy, Jean (who would benefit most from his death) secretly releases him. Javert, stunned that Jean could be merciful even to him and tormented by the fact that he did not deserve Jean's forgiveness, kills himself.

Suggestions for Viewing

Les Miserables does not drag, although it is quite long. But because of the intensity of the movie, it may be wise to show it on consecutive nights rather than at one sitting. Nothing in the movie is offensive.

Important Scenes and/or Quotes

When Jean first enters the priest's home he is offered food and a bed.

> **Jean:** I can't pay for this!
> **Priest:** This isn't my house; it is the house of Christ. No, do not thank me. You are more at home here than myself. And all that is in here is yours.
> **Jean:** You don't even know who I am.
> **Priest:** You're my brother and I can tell that you have suffered greatly.

Jean has set Javert free. As the revolutionaries are being overtaken by the government forces, Jean attempts to escape through the sewers. Javert follows him.

> **Javert:** Why did you let me go?
> **Jean:** I had no choice.

Javert: Choice?

Jean: Once, many years ago, a remarkable man bought my soul. He removed from it all evil thoughts and gave it to God.

Javert: There is no God. There is only the law. Guilt and innocence do not exist outside the law.

Jean: If that is what you believe, then you must kill me. Kill me now!

Discussion Questions

How was Jean bought with a price? How did it change him? Why?

How have we been bought with a price? How should it change us?

If there were no God, would what Javert thought about forgiveness be true (that is, there is no need for mercy)? What did Javert discover?

To what extent have we been forgiven? Are there things for which we cannot be forgiven?

If we have been treated with mercy, how should we treat others? How much should we forgive others?

Outline of Talk or Wrap-up

Use *Les Miserables* for a discussion on forgiveness.

Explain that the forgiveness offered to Jean by the priest mirrors the forgiveness God extends to us. Jean was guilty but the priest forgave him and even offered him more. We stand guilty before God, but he forgives us and supplies blessings without number.

State that though the price for the priest was relatively minor, the price God paid for our forgiveness was the death of his Son. The worth of our forgiveness is obvious when we see how greatly God loved the Son whom he gave up for us.

Emphasize the need for every individual to ask God for the forgiveness he offers.

Make it clear that since we have been forgiven our lives should also mirror the forgiveness God shows. Our relationships should be characterized by mercy.

Related Bible References

Psalm 130:4 (forgiveness is from God); Ephesians 1:7 (forgiveness is through death of Jesus); Colossians 3:13 (we need to forgive as God forgave us); Matthew 18 (how many times to forgive).

Other Ideas

Les Miserables could be used in a study that compares justice and compassion and when both are appropriate. It is also a good example of a life that is controlled by unselfish love.

Jared Reed

38

The Lords of Discipline

- R
- 103 minutes
- A 1983 film based on the novel by Pat Conroy

Synopsis and Review

The Lords of Discipline is the account of Will McClean's (David Keith) senior year at the Carolina Military Institute. The Institute's code of honor is short and sweet: "Students will not lie, cheat, steal or tolerate those who do." Its goal is nothing less than making "men of iron," capable of leadership.

It is 1964, and this school steeped in Southern tradition has admitted its first black student, Pearce (Mark Breland) into its freshman class. McClean's commandant and mentor, Bear (Robert Prosky), assigns him the responsibility of watching out for Pearce. Will's three roommates, Mark (John Lavachelli), Pig (Rick Rossovich), and Trad (Mitchell Lichtenstein) are not entirely thrilled with this assignment, questioning both his motivation and friendship.

Pearce survives the most intense hazing the school has to offer—"hell night." Unfortunately this doesn't please everyone and a group known only as "The Ten" emerge to torment him and drive him out of the school. They threaten Pearce by telling him, "You're going on a ride. You're going down the hole; and if you ever get out alive, you'll wish you were dead." Seeing this as unjust, Will sets out to unravel the mystery of The Ten, who as the legend has it are supposedly the ten finest cadets in the school. In the process, he comes face to face with the reality that the very institution he has come to respect is also the power behind The Ten. Ultimately this forces him to decide to risk

155

all (graduation, respect, and friendship) to do what he knows is right. Mark and Pig stand by him. Trad, who as it turns out is a secret member of The Ten, is hesitant to get involved. Pig is expelled. Mark and Will face expulsion as the demerit system is turned against them. In the end, Will makes a deal with General Durrell (G. D. Spradlin), the head of the school, by threatening to expose the heavy-handed practices of the Institute.

Suggestions for Viewing

Lords is a powerful dramatization of life in a military institution. Much of what makes this movie powerful is the plot building, suspense, and resolution of crisis. However *Lords* does contain strong language and suggestive content that may be objectionable. Definitely preview this movie before showing it in its entirety. Below are several select scenes and quotes that could be used as discussion starters or illustrations.

Important Scenes and/or Quotes

1. Will is asked why he is protecting Pearce to which he answers, "Because it's right."
2. General Durrell reads the telegram communicating the death of his son to the members of the senior class. It briefly tells of his accidental death, ending with the line, "He was a fine soldier."
3. Will, expressing to Bear his disillusion with the Institute says, "If ten guys can go around in the dark, change the rules anytime they want and get away with it . . . if that's the honor of this institute, that ring (the school ring) is a piece of crap."
4. Pig's appearance in honor court, the misuse of the honor code against him, and his walk of shame.
5. Will's confrontation with Trad. Trad tells him that becoming a member of the ten is the only thing he's done on his own. It meant something to his father.
6. Pearce's explanation of why he didn't corroborate Will's accusation against the ten: "I'm the first. If I don't make it, the next nigger has my mark around his neck like a rock."

7. Bear's tossing Will his school ring that he left behind, "Take it; you earned it."

Discussion Questions

What is the purpose of the honor code? How is this original purpose violated by the very institution that it is supposed to support?

Why does Will defend Pearce? What would you have done?

What makes people prejudiced? Why is prejudice such a powerful motivation? In what ways do you prejudge people?

What is the purpose of tradition? How important is tradition? When should traditions be challenged? Why is that difficult?

Why did Trad want to be part of The Ten? What was his motivation?

In what ways did Will's experience benefit him or make him a better person?

Outline of Talk or Wrap-up

Ultimately *Lords* is about having the courage to do what is right, even when the consequences are unpleasant. This movie could be used to encourage believers to do right despite the circumstances. Different areas of peer pressure that the members of your group face could be explored. Discuss why it's easier just to go with the crowd rather than stand up for what is right (we want acceptance and fear rejection). Some sub-themes that could be explored are:

1. The contrast between Will and Trad. Will was willing to do what was right despite the possible consequences. Trad, on the other hand, was a compromiser who was more interested in gaining his father's approval than doing right.
2. The issue of racism and prejudice; and
3. Friendship.

Related Bible References

Daniel 3; Daniel 7:16–28 (examples of Shadrach, Meshach, Abednego, and Daniel doing what was right regardless of the consequences); John 15:18–20 (promise of trials for followers of Christ); James 1:2–4 (benefit of trials); John 4:4–30 (Jesus' example of overcoming Jewish prejudice against Samaritans); and Proverbs 18:24; 27:6; Ecclesiastes 4:10 (importance of friendship).

Robert Eugene DiPaolo

39

Mask

- PG-13
- 120 minutes
- A 1985 film

Synopsis and Review

Rocky Dennis was a bright, lovable, cheerful sixteen-year-old who loved baseball cards, Harley-Davidsons, and reading books about faraway places. He also had a face that looked like something you might see at a carnival sideshow. Rocky suffered from neuromyofibrosis, a disease that caused the bones in his head to grow to grotesque proportions—making it seem as though he were wearing a hideous mask. *Mask* is the story of one year of Rocky's life, based on the true account of the real-life Rocky Dennis.

Mask opens with Rocky's (Eric Stoltz) excitement and apprehension over enrolling in a new school, a frightening enough prospect for any teenager, much less one who looks like the lead character in a monster movie. Rocky's mom, Rusty Dennis (Cher), is a free spirit with lots of rough edges, but she makes up for it in her fierce devotion to her son. The film revolves around Rocky's attempts to be a normal teenager, as a student, friend, baseball fan, and young guy trying to figure out girls, in spite of his looks. His relationship with his mom and her various boyfriends (especially Gar, played by Sam Elliott), and her drug problem, form the major sub-plots. The acting is terrific; the movie never drags, and it grabs your heartstrings the whole way through.

Suggestions for Viewing

Mask needs to be seen as a whole to really get the message. This presents a problem because the movie is filled with profanity and some suggested sexual situations (not very explicit). But the moral of the story is so appropriate for kids that I think it's worth taking the risk and showing in its entirety. I suggest you preview it, see what it's about (keep a box of tissues handy), and send advise/consent forms home for the parents to sign if they will permit their kids to see it.

Important Scenes and/or Quotes

If you decide to show just selected scenes, here are three that stand out:

1. At approximately fifteen to twenty minutes into the movie, we see and hear Rocky's worries about being accepted at his new school, and then the actual first day. Anyone who has ever suffered from "newschoolaphobia" will sweat along with him; anyone who is insecure about his/her looks, will die inside vicariously. In other words, everyone will relate.
2. At the twenty-six minute mark, Rocky and Rusty have a pretty heavy confrontation over Rusty's drug abuse and social life. There's a lot of profanity, but the dialogue is powerful and will definitely hit home with kids who have similar struggles with their parents (an alarmingly large and rapidly increasing group.)
3. At about one hour and fifteen minutes, there is a touching sequence about Rocky's work as a counselor at a camp for the blind. It is sadly ironic that Rocky experiences so much more acceptance there than anywhere else, leaving you to wonder who's really blind. He also falls in love here; those scenes are very touching.

Discussion Questions

Better than any movie I've seen in a long time, *Mask* raises the question about just what makes a person valuable. What gives us worth, dignity, self-esteem? In this film, it's obvious that for most people, the answer is—loudly and clearly and before all else—what we look like.

Mask does an excellent job of showing us a person who has incredible inner beauty and dignity, despite his external appearance. (In fact, if I had to criticize the movie at all, and it is a very minor criticism, I might wonder if the movie didn't make Rocky a little too saintly.) This film should definitely spark a productive discussion of self-image, self-esteem, human dignity, etc.

As a secondary theme, you could explore the interesting role reversal that takes place between son and mother: Rocky often acting more like the parent, and Rusty like the rebellious, irresponsible child. Again, it is an unfortunate fact of our culture that you will in all likelihood have kids in your group who are experiencing that in their homes.

Another worthwhile theme (related to the first) is that of acceptance. What people accept and love Rocky for who he is? Almost without exception, it is the outcasts of society: the prostitute, the bikers, the losers. The same is undoubtedly true of the schools that your kids attend. The outcasts tend to accept people just as they are, no hoops to jump through, no social points to keep track of. If Jesus went to Rocky's school, how would he treat Rocky? If Jesus went to your kids' school(s), whom would he hang out with? What implications does this have for the social, class structure your kids deal with?

Outline of Talk or Wrap-up

Mask makes a powerful, intense statement about what makes us valuable and worthwhile as human beings. In this movie, it's obvious that Rocky Dennis is one terrific guy, and everyone who watches it will fall in love with him and identify strongly with his hurts, pains, and triumphs. And yet, if another "Rocky" were to suddenly show up at your youth group meeting, would he/she be treated with compassion and acceptance? Why is it we're so prejudiced by other people's (and consumed with our own) appearances?

This film offers a very valuable insight into true dignity, etc. The Bible teaches that our worth and dignity come from being made in the image of God and being redeemed through the death of Christ. Use *Mask* to help your kids get beyond shallow and superficial thinking about human value, self-esteem, etc.

Related Bible References

Genesis 1:26–31; Psalm 8:3–9; John 3:16; Romans 5:6–8; Romans 8:31–39.

Kent Keller

40

The Mission

- PG
- 130 minutes
- A 1986 film

Synopsis and Review

A cinematic masterpiece, *The Mission* is a visually compelling film. Shot on location in Brazil, with a superb cast and a stunning musical score, *The Mission* will be remembered long after the credits roll by.

Robert DeNiro as Rodrigo Mendoza and Jeremy Irons as Father Gabriel play the lead roles in this depiction of religious politics during the colonization of South America. After a rough start, a group of priests begins a mission among an Indian tribe, the Guaraní, in a politically disputed area. Altamirano (Ray McAnally), a representative of the church, must decide whether the mission can continue, or if the land will be turned over to the Spaniards or Portuguese—the latter being the "politically wise" choice.

The story centers around a Jesuit priest, Father Gabriel, who is evangelizing the native Indians and has built a mission, and Rodrigo Mendoza, a slave trader. In a tragic turn of events during an argument, Mendoza accidentally kills his brother. Filled with remorse and guilt, he is convinced that he is beyond salvation. Through Father Gabriel (his former enemy), Mendoza finds God's grace and forgiveness and becomes a Jesuit.

Eventually the two men must decide how to respond to the order of the church and the state, to close the mission and thus open the area and the Indians to slavery again.

The strong themes of *The Mission* are cultural prejudice, grace, and responding to violence and injustice.

163

Suggestions for Viewing

This is a very powerful film when viewed in its entirety. However, a few scenes, with a little setup, would be good discussion starters shown by themselves. These are outlined below.

Warning: The movie contains realistic, shocking violence. Scores of Indians, including women and children, are shot. There is also some nudity because of the tribal setting.

Important Scenes and/or Quotes

1. At about twenty minutes into the film, after Rodrigo has killed his brother, he takes up residence in a monastery and is unable to forgive himself. Father Gabriel challenges him to do whatever is necessary to find forgiveness, suggesting he choose his own penance.

   Rodrigo responds that he is beyond forgiveness. But when Father Gabriel challenges Rodrigo, accusing him of fear, Rodrigo agrees to work out his forgiveness, doing the penance that Father Gabriel designs.

   This penance involves a seemingly impossible task. Rodrigo must accompany Father Gabriel on his return to the new mission, climbing up the side of a two-hundred-foot waterfall while carrying a huge bundle of armor, weapons, and other remnants from his past.

   Finally, the tortured climb ends when they reach the top. But then Rodrigo is confronted by the Guaraní Indians who recognize him as the one who had enslaved and killed their people. In a dramatic moment, an Indian approaches Rodrigo with a knife. But then, instead of exacting revenge and killing him, the Indian cuts off the bundle and pushes it over the edge of the cliff, into the river below. At that, Rodrigo Mendoza, the hardened, tough slave trader, who is filled with guilt and shame, breaks down and weeps uncontrollably. He could not find forgiveness through works, no matter how difficult his penance—only through grace.

2. The second good discussion starter happens fifteen minutes from the end of the film. Spain and Portugal have adjusted their territorial claims in the Treaty of Madrid, turning several Jesuit missions in South America over to

Portuguese rule. The Portuguese order Gabriel and Rodrigo to evacuate. This means the mission will be dismantled because the Portuguese want the Indians as slaves. Some of the priests, led by Rodrigo (who has joined the order), plan to fight the takeover. Gabriel refuses, insisting that, since God is love, fighting is wrong.

Begin when Rodrigo comes into Gabriel's hut for a blessing. The following is their interchange:

Rodrigo: Father, I've come to ask you to bless me.
Gabriel: No. If you're right, you'll have God's blessing. If you're wrong, my blessing won't mean anything. If might is right, then love has no place in the world. That may be so, that may be so. . . . But I don't have the strength to live in a world like that, Rodrigo. I can't bless you.

Discussion Questions

For the first scene:

Why did Rodrigo think he was beyond forgiveness?
What did Gabriel tell him to do to be forgiven?
What good did Rodrigo's penance do for him?
What does the word "grace" mean?
How did the Indian demonstrate grace to Rodrigo?
Why do you think the Indian cut the rope?
How is this scene a picture of what God does for us?
According to the Bible, how does someone receive God's forgiveness?

For the second suggested scene:

Whose reaction to the army do you agree with: Gabriel's or Rodrigo's? Why?
How would you combine the biblical command to love with the view many Christians hold, that war is appropriate when defending freedom?
How does God want you to react to your enemies?

Outline of Talk or Wrap-up

1. God's Grace

   All have sinned, and all are guilty. Some may have sinned more than others, but all of us deserve God's death penalty.

   People respond in various ways to their sin and guilt. Some try to deny it; some try to work it out; some, like Rodrigo Mendoza, feel unforgivable and hate themselves.

   The good news is that we can be forgiven. No matter what we have done, we can find forgiveness and salvation . . . but not by works, only through grace.

   Grace is "undeserved favor." Like Mendoza, we deserve death for our sins. But, like the Indian, God cuts the rope and sets us free from our burden of sin when we come to him in repentance and faith.

2. Violence vs. Nonviolent Response

   Talk about love and war. Refer to the Crusades and other times when Christians have fought for God (whether wrongly or rightly). If you can pull it off, it would be great to have two articulate and knowledgeable Christians debate this subject.

Related Bible References

On grace and forgiveness: Micah 7:18; Luke 7:39–50; Joel 2:12–13; Romans 5:8; 1 John 1:9. On love and war: 1 John 3:11–14; 1 John 3:1–3; 1 Corinthians 10:24; Ephesians 5:1–2.

Other Ideas

Show the courtyard trial scene (right in the middle of the movie) and discuss cultural prejudice and stereotypes.

Use *The Mission* during your church's missions festival to set up a discussion on missions in general, or on the concept of culturalization specifically.

Mark Oestreicher

41

The Money Pit

- PG
- 91 minutes
- A 1986 film

Synopsis and Review

Shelley Long (as Anna Crowley) and Tom Hanks (as Walter Fielding) star in this comedy about a couple searching for their dream house. After looking for some time, they locate an old house that needs "minor repairs." One thing after another goes wrong, hence the title. These catastrophes can be somewhat silly, but most of them offer good comic interpretations of classic house problems. Hanks, with his unique physical comedy style, adds much to the film.

Suggestions for Viewing

The only reason I've suggested this video is for one very funny scene. Its potential use is described below.

Warning: *The Money Pit* has some swearing and a couple of sexually suggestive scenes. The scene outlined contains no swearing or sexual references.

Important Scenes and/or Quotes

The usable scene can be found approximately one hour into the film. If you fast forward, look for Tom Hanks carrying a small metal bucket around the house (he's trying to get some water for Anna). Explain the basic premise of the scene before showing it. There's no need to explain the plot of the movie for this one.

This scene is an exaggerated, slapstick demonstration of Murphy's Law (everything that can go wrong will go wrong). One accident sets off another, and another, and another—all in comic succession. Start the scene from where Anna discovers that water actually comes out of the faucet. Stop the scene when the garden fountain douses Walter (Tom Hanks). Use this funny clip to set up a talk on "When everything seems to go wrong."

Discussion Questions

Have you ever felt as though your life is out of control?

Think of the last time you had a day when nothing seemed to go right. What happened?

When things aren't going well in your life, how do you feel about God?

Why does God sometimes seem to be silent when things get tough?

Outline of Talk or Wrap-up

After showing the scene and working through the discussion questions, talk to the students about God's omniscience. Refer to his care for the sparrows and how much more he cares for us. Also explain that we need faith, even in times when God doesn't seem to be there. Because God knows everything, and he cares about us so much, his plans for us are always good (even if we don't understand what's going on).

Caution: this is not a simple subject. If you talk to students about this type of subject, be prepared! Today's teens deal with hard adult issues. Many have already struggled with depression and the feeling of desertion by God. Don't gloss over their concerns with overly-simplistic answers.

Related Bible References

Matthew 10:29–31 (the sparrow passage); Isaiah 40:13–14; John 2:24; Psalm 147:5.

Other Ideas

Parents may decide to watch the entire film with their kids. If so, go ahead and take advantage of the other topics covered. Talk about the importance of trust in relationships. You may also want to discuss materialism.

Mark Oestreicher

42

Mr. Mom

- PG
- 92 minutes
- A 1983 film

Synopsis and Review

This movie takes an amusing look at role reversal:
What happens when Dad unexpectedly loses his job, Mom
becomes the breadwinner, and Dad finds himself at home,
raising kids and running a household full-time?

Though the plot is somewhat predictable, this film contains some genuinely funny moments. Michael Keaton
plays Jack, the laid-off auto designer who must now battle
runaway vacuum cleaners and overflowing washing
machines. Teri Garr is Caroline, the former housewife suddenly thrust into the "life in the fast lane" corporate world
of advertising. The reversal of roles sparks major tension
both *within* the characters and *between* them.

The movie has a happy, slapstick ending in which both
Jack and Caroline resist the temptation to engage in adul-
terous relationships. The characters emerge with dignity,
stronger and closer as a result of their trials.

Suggestions for Viewing

The most powerful scene in *Mr. Mom* occurs in the final
ten minutes of the film. This final scene can stand alone if
a brief synopsis is given first and if the last scene is set up
as outlined below.

Mr. Mom is a very clean film, with only an occasional
swear word.

Important Scenes and/or Quotes

Joan is a sexy neighbor who has been seeking an opportunity to seduce Jack.

The moment finally comes when Jack goes upstairs to shower. Joan follows quietly, drinks in hand. As Jack is shaving, Joan (Ann Jillian) calls out from the bedroom. Jack simultaneously feels fear, shock, and sexual temptation. Talking to himself in the mirror, he begins to list the arguments for and against an affair:

> All right, A: She's an attractive woman.
> B: She wants you, Jack . . . she wants you *bad*.
> C: I don't even want to think about C!
> D: Kenny'd talk. Alex, Alex would be okay. Kenny'd talk. He'd crack.

After cutting away to other action, the camera comes back to Jack still listing the pros and cons of an affair with Joan.

> M: I'm a free agent!
> N: I could be in the middle of it, I could have a heart attack, I could die. Caroline walks in, sees me here. I die *and* get caught!

After another cutaway, the camera returns to a steam-filled bathroom in time to hear Jack say:

> Y: Why did I get rid of that woobie? (a reference to his son's security blanket)
> Z: *You're not going to do anything, because you, my friend, are in love with your wife!* (emphasis added)

Discussion Questions

Do you tend to think long and hard about each temptation that comes your way? Or do you tend to react impulsively? Which is safer? Why?

We Christians often sin even when we know better and try really hard not to, sometimes even though we are aware that our disobedience may have serious consequences. We disobey despite Scripture memory, accountability, fervent prayer, and all our resolutions and promises to God. Why?

What is it about love that can keep us faithful (whether in a human relationship or in our walk with God)?

How might your relationship with God be different, if you answered your temptation as Jack answered his? "You're not going to do that because you, _____ , are in love with your Lord Jesus Christ and your number one goal is to please him."

How does this kind of faithful love develop and grow?

Outline of Talk or Wrap-up

Use this powerful scene from *Mr. Mom* to wrap up a talk or discussion on how to resist temptation or how to overcome stubborn sins.

Explain to students that sin is not just breaking an abstract, impersonal set of laws, but it is breaking the heart of God. Drive home the fact that he is wounded by our unfaithfulness just as we would be hurt if a mate ignored our feelings and took up with someone else.

Emphasize that fear is an inadequate motivation for obedience and self-effort is an impotent means for avoiding sin. Only love can prompt genuine God-honoring obedience.

Related Bible References

John 14:15, 21; 1 John 5:3 (obeying God out of love for God); 2 Corinthians 5:9, 14 (pleasing God because of love for God); Hosea (How sin breaks the heart of God, and how a relationship with God means faithfully loving him).

Other Ideas

Mr. Mom can also be used to discuss sexual roles (*see* Eph. 5 and 6): what tasks and responsibilities Christian husbands and wives should assume.

Len Woods

43

Mr. Smith Goes to Washington

- Unrated
- 129 minutes
- A 1939 film

Synopsis and Review

This film, starring Jimmy Stewart as Jefferson Smith and Jean Arthur as Clarissa Saunders, is about an idealistic young man who comes face-to-face with governmental corruption when he is appointed to the United States Senate.

Senator Samuel Foley dies with two months left in his term. Every special interest group in the state is pressuring Governor Hubert Hopper (Guy Kibbe) to appoint their man. The heaviest influence comes from Senator Joseph Paine (Claude Rains) and Jim Taylor (Edward Arnold), a newspaper publisher who "owns and controls" Paine and numerous other politicians.

Taylor and Paine want an appointee who will take orders and not make waves . . . especially since Paine has introduced legislation to build the Willet Creek Dam, a project that will put millions in the pocket of Taylor, and that Paine is pushing in exchange for Taylor's future support in getting onto the National ticket.

In what he thinks is a brilliant (and independent) stroke of political genius, Governor Hopper appoints Jefferson Smith, leader of the Boy Rangers, (an organization similar to the Boy Scouts) to fill the Senate term. Smith is something of a state hero, having recently put out a raging forest fire. He also is a "big-eyed patriot [who] knows Washington and Lincoln by heart." Hopper feels that Smith can be controlled easily and that his popularity back home will mean votes at election time.

The plan backfires. With the help of Clarissa Saunders, a shrewd young legislative secretary, Smith draws up a bill for a National Boys Camp on the very land that Paine and Taylor have eyed for the Willet Creek Dam!

A tremendous "David vs. Goliath" struggle ensues. Taylor's powerful political machine seeks to destroy Smith even as he fights for what is right and decent. Smith, with Saunders' assistance, launches a filibuster that is mesmerizing.

In the end, Smith's words finally pierce Senator Paine's heart. He admits the Willet Creek Dam scam. David has defeated Goliath!

Suggestions for Viewing

Since it appears on almost every critic's list of the "all-time greatest movies," *Mr. Smith Goes to Washington* ought to be viewed in its entirety by everyone! If you don't have the time, however, at least watch the scenes in which Taylor and Paine try to convince Smith to "come on board" and Smith's filibuster in the Senate.

Important Scenes and/or Quotes

Immediately after Smith is appointed to office, he and Senator Paine discuss Clayton Smith, Jefferson's father, who was a friend of Paine's.

Jefferson:	Yeah, Dad always used to say the only causes worth fighting for were lost causes.
Paine:	You don't have to tell me, Jeff. We were a team, the two of us, a struggling editor and a struggling lawyer. The twin champions of lost causes, they used to call us.
Jefferson:	Ma's told me about it a thousand times.
Paine:	His last fight was his best, Jeff. He and his little four-page paper against that mining syndicate and all to defend the right of one small miner who stuck to his

claim. You know, they tried everything, bribery, intimidation, then . . . well. . . .

Jefferson: Yes, Ma found him slumped over his desk that morning. . . .

Paine: Shot in the back. I was there. I can see him at that old rolltop desk, still with his hat on . . . still with his hat on.

Jefferson: I know. I suppose, Mr. Paine, when a fellow bucks up against a big organization like that, one man by himself can't get far, can he?

Paine: No.

Then, at the end of the movie, twenty-four hours into his filibuster, his voice nearly gone, Jefferson Smith stares at the piles of telegrams against him and declares:

I guess this is just another lost cause, Mr. Paine. All you people don't know about lost causes. Mr. Paine does. He said once they were the only causes worth fighting for, and he fought for them once, for the only reason that any man ever fights for them. Because of just one plain, simple rule, "Love thy neighbor," and in this world today, full of hatred, a man who knows that one rule has a great trust. You knew that rule, Mr. Paine, and I loved you for it, just as my father did. And you know that you fight for the lost causes harder than for any others. Yes, you'd even die for them, like a man we both know, Mr. Paine. You think I'm licked. You all think I'm licked. Well, I'm not licked and I'm going to stay right here and fight for this lost cause even if this room gets filled with lies like these, and the Taylors and all their armies come marching into this place. Somebody'll listen to me . . . some. . . .

At this point, Jefferson faints, and Paine, pierced by the truth, admits his own wrongdoing.

Discussion Questions

How much corruption do you think goes on in government?

How can a godly man or woman become immersed in politics and not compromise his or her integrity?

If you had two months to serve as a high-ranking government official, what would you try to accomplish and why?

How willing are you to stand up for what is right? Could you (*would you*) endure losing friends, being laughed at, being called names, being ridiculed or slandered, being physically threatened?

Whom do you admire most in this film and why?

If Christians approached their assignment to spread the gospel as eagerly as Jefferson Smith approached writing his bill, how would the world be different? Why are we often so unexcited about spreading our faith?

Was Jefferson Smith a true leader? Why or why not?

Outline of Talk or Wrap-up
What Makes a Leader?

1. Love (1 Cor. 13:4–8)
2. Enthusiasm (2 Cor. 8:17)
3. Accountability (James 5:16)
4. Discipline (Phil. 3)
5. Encouragement (1 Thess. 5:11)
6. Respectability (1 Tim. 3:2)

Related Bible References

First Samuel 17 tells the story of David and Goliath. Numbers 13—14 describe Joshua and Caleb standing alone against the other ten spies and all the children of Israel. Daniel is a great book about integrity and refusal to compromise; see chapter 1 for the story of Daniel's unwillingness to eat the king's food. See chapter 3 for the story about the three Hebrew youths in the fiery furnace and chapter 6 for Daniel's boldness in praying to Yahweh despite the decree of the Persian king.

Other Ideas

Use *Mr. Smith Goes to Washington* to talk about the issues of character and/or reputation; use it at a youth meeting on or around Independence Day.

Len Woods

44
The Natural

- PG
- 134 minutes
- A 1984 film version of the Bernard Malamud novel

Synopsis and Review

This drama centers around Roy Hobbs (Robert Redford), a young farm boy who seems to have been created to be a baseball player (hence the name, "The Natural.") The plot develops along these lines:

Through his God-given abilities and hard work, Roy's baseball talents pay off and he is called up for a tryout with a major league team. On the way to the tryout, through some interesting twists of fate involving "The Whammer" (Joe Don Baker), a Babe Ruth caricature, and Harriet Bird (Barbara Hershey), a psychotic woman bent on destroying great athletes (and herself), Roy's seemingly smooth ride to the big time is derailed. He disappears for sixteen years.

He then is discovered playing minor league ball by a scout for a major league team (the New York Knights). He gets called up to the majors, but meets with nothing but obstacles, primarily in the form of a manager, Pop Fisher (Wilford Brimley), who can't believe he's been sent a thirty-five-year-old "rookie." He doesn't even give Roy a chance until fate intervenes (the starting right fielder is killed) and he has to play Roy. Roy immediately begins tearing up the league, hitting monstrous home runs and leading the Knights out of the cellar and into the pennant race. All is going great for Roy until another woman, Memo Paris

(Kim Basinger), enters his life, and Roy's life takes a drastic turn for the worse.

But you can't keep a good man down. Yet another woman, Iris Gaines (Glenn Close), who had been Roy's childhood sweetheart, reenters the picture, symbolizing everything good about life, baseball, the American way, etc. Roy's career rebounds, and the Knights find themselves in a one-game playoff for the pennant. Roy comes back from his deathbed to save the game for the Knights, for Pop Fisher, and for the forces of good. I'm overstating the symbolism a little, but not much.

Suggestions for Viewing

The Natural is probably too long for many, if not most teenagers to sit through without getting antsy. So there are some scenes described below that could be used effectively to start discussions and/or illustrate principles that you could build on.

There's very little in *The Natural* that will offend the average American teenager. You could probably show the entire film to most groups without their noticing anything objectionable. But you might be concerned over the occasional profanity, particularly the use of God's name as such. There are also one or two suggested sexual situations, but they are pretty mild compared to what can be seen anytime on network television. That doesn't mean it's OK; it just means it won't shock most kids.

Important Scenes and/or Quotes and Discussion Questions

The first such scene occurs approximately twenty-five minutes into the movie when the evil Harriet first approaches young Roy on the train on the way to his major league tryout. After she asks him about his abilities and his intentions, the conversation continues:

> **Harriet:** What will you hope to accomplish?
> **Roy:** When I walk down the street, people will look at me and say, There goes Roy Hobbs, the best there ever was.
> **Harriet:** Is that all?
> **Roy:** Well, what else is there?

Harriet: Don't you know? Isn't there something more? More
glorious?

What follows tells us that Roy is to be a tragic hero; but you
could stop the film and ask about the group members' motivation in life, in school, in sports, in work. Is it just to get by, to get
out, to get a letter or a paycheck? Or are they driven to be the
best they could possibly be at a particular calling?

Then you may want to follow up on Harriet's question: "Is
that all?", followed by Roy's: "Well, what else is there?"

Another applicable scene occurs about three-quarters of the
way into the movie. Roy has been hospitalized because of his
old wound (suffered at the hands of Harriet) and has been told
he will be risking his life if he ever plays baseball again. Several
subplots are important here: Roy's bad judgment (sin?) involving Harriet has come back to haunt him; his team is facing the
one game playoff for the pennant, and they are bound to lose
without him; and the judge (Robert Prosky), the symbol of utter
evil in the film, has come to Roy's bedside to bribe him into not
playing, thus assuring the Knights losing, or he (the judge) will
reveal the sordid episode involving Harriet to the public. Several
questions could be raised here:

If you were Roy, what would you do? Would you risk your life
to play one last (very important) game?

Knowing that baseball players didn't make the kind of
money back then that they do now, why shouldn't Roy
take the large amount of money ($20,000) the judge was
offering him so he could walk away from baseball financially set for life and get the girl (his childhood sweetheart)
as a bonus?

Playing baseball again meant risking the judge's exposure of
Roy's tragic past. Not only would that be personally humil-
iating, but it would also disillusion the millions of kids who
idolize Roy. What part should that have in his decision to
play or not to play?

There's one more very poignant and, for the plot's purposes,
significant scene about ten minutes before the movie ends. Roy
has come back from the hospital to play the last game. He sur-

prises Pop Fisher as he gets ready for the game. In essence, Pop tells Roy he is the best player he's ever managed and the best hitter he's ever seen, thus fulfilling Roy's dream of being called "the best there ever was." Unfortunately, Pop says this while using God's name in vain, which renders this scene unusable, unless you're dealing with mature kids.

If you do choose to show the whole film, look for the following themes and/or symbols: the presence of the supernatural (manifested by lightning) at several pivotal points in Roy's life; the contrast between good/evil, light/dark, white/black (what the various women wear, the judge's office, the climactic scene when Roy's home run blast shatters the lights and ends the game in a shower of sparks).

Outline of Talk or Wrap-up

This movie paints some powerful images that could easily be the starting point for productive discussions. If your teenagers are like the ones I've known, they don't genuinely understand that actions have consequences. They don't realize that cheating in school now and promiscuous behavior now have unfortunate consequences later. Roy's one great mistake (there are smaller ones, but they don't come into view as prominently) in "flirting" with Harriet turned out to be disastrous. What "paths" are your young people on now? Where will those paths lead? It's much easier to correct them now than it will be later.

Related Bible References

See Genesis 16 (the story of Abram's unfaithfulness with Hagar, and the difficulties that have come about through the two lineages ever since); Genesis 37—50 (the stories of Joseph and his brothers); 2 Samuel 11—24 (the stories of David's adultery with Bathsheba and the troubles that followed—chapters 11 and 12 deal specifically with David and Bathsheba and the death of their child). For the light vs. dark theme, the book of 1 John would be very appropriate, as well as the great prologue in John 1:1–18.

Kent Keller

45
Never Cry Wolf

- PG
- 105 minutes
- A 1983 film

Synopsis and Review

Never Cry Wolf is a fairly straightforward drama about a man against the elements. The elements in this case are wolves and the Alaskan wilderness. As it turns out, it is not an adversarial relationship.

An absolutely green and unprepared scientist, Tyler (Charles Martin Smith) is sent out into the Alaskan tundra to study wolves. He knows a lot about wolves in a clinical way, but nothing at all about them in their natural environment, nor how to cope with that environment himself as he attempts to observe them. His struggles to survive and carry out his mission give the film its dynamic tension and more than a little comic relief.

Suggestions for Viewing

This film is not long, so you could show it in its entirety. Because one of the major themes is the transformation of Tyler (from completely incapable of dealing with the wilderness to very much at home there), it may be that you will need to show it all. There's enough beautiful scenery to keep everyone's interest.

There is another contrast that can best be appreciated by watching the whole movie. Notice the seemingly utter remoteness of the area where Tyler observes the wolves, and compare that with the scene near the end where the three bozos appear who want to develop the area and turn

181

it into a resort. One of the three, Rosie (Brian Dennehy), is a roguish bush pilot we meet in one of the earlier scenes. His transformation from a bumbling but lovable adventurer into a cynical profiteer is especially troubling.

Warnings: There is some profanity in this film. Also, some may be offended by the "territory-marking" scene; and there are a couple of scenes that show Tyler naked—in one he is jumping into a lake for a bath; in the other he is running through a herd of caribou (honest). Neither scene can be considered remotely erotic, nor are they particularly explicit, but you should definitely preview to determine whether this is appropriate for your kids.

Important Scenes and/or Quotes and Discussion Questions

There are a few scenes in *Never Cry Wolf* that stand out as particularly interesting.

1. The entire episode when Rosie flies Tyler to his base camp (practically at the beginning of the film) is funny and entertaining. Take note of the cinematography as Tyler watches Rosie fly off into the Alaskan sky, leaving him totally alone and isolated in a very unforgiving environment. You could ask your group questions like, "When have you experienced feelings of isolation like Tyler did at that point?"

2. Another possibility occurs shortly after that, when the "wolves" come and Tyler hides from them, only to discover that he's being rescued by an Indian and his sled dogs. Ootek (Zachary Ittimangnaq) motions for Tyler to come with him, and Tyler has to leave behind much of his valuable equipment and supplies. Ask: "If you were in that situation, what would you take with you? What would you leave behind? When it's survival, what is really important? Even though we are not in a 'survival' situation, what's really important for us?"

3. The episode showing Tyler marking his territory wolf-style is very funny, and, if your group is mature enough, could be used in the following way. Ask: "How do we

show that we are also territorial creatures by nature? What happens when you feel someone is invading your space?"

4. Approximately an hour into the film, Tyler gives a short soliloquy where he ponders why he has always been an observer instead of a participant. It could be very revealing to ask whether your kids consider themselves observers or participants in life. In our video-conscious, television-oriented culture, this is a loaded question, one that could have broad implications for the way our kids (and we) live—as spectators or players. Christianity calls for involvement; television, movies, and videos almost dictate detached, passive non-involvement. The choice is ours. Think this through before you take this approach—it could be a very powerful discussion, and you want to make sure it takes a positive direction.

5. There's one last scene that might stir up some strong emotions, especially if your group has some "save the whales" types. At approximately one hour and twenty minutes into the film, Tyler and Mike (Samson Jorah) discuss whether or not it would be OK to kill wolves for their fur. Mike thinks it would be all right; Tyler doesn't say, but you know he's become attached to the wolves he's been observing and wouldn't kill them. What do your kids think? Is it OK to kill animals to survive? Or just because you like their fur?

   Of course, many (if not most) of your kids will probably say it is wrong. If you like playing devil's advocate, ask them if they eat hamburgers and other kinds of meat, wear leather shoes, carry leather handbags, etc.

6. *Never Cry Wolf* ends with an "Old Innuit [Indian] Song" that is thought-provoking and open to interesting interpretation:

> I think over again my small adventures.
> My Fears,
> Those small ones that seemed so big.
> For all the vital things
> I had to get and to reach.
> And yet there is only one great thing,
> The only thing.

To live to see the great day that dawns
And the light that fills the world.

Outline of Talk or Wrap-up

This movie works on several levels, the two most important being Tyler's transformation from incompetent to one-with-the-elements; and also the struggle of progress (?) versus nature. You could use the first to talk about conversion in a couple of different ways (spiritual, emotional maturation, learning to take responsibility for ourselves, etc.)

The second is an issue with which we and our children will be struggling for the rest of our lives. (Think Exxon-Valdez and Prince William Sound; Saddam Hussein and the ecological terrorism in the Kuwaiti oil fields; toxic wastes showing up on the beaches of the East coast of the United States.)

Related Bible References

See Genesis 1:26–31—the creation of man and the mandate to subdue all creation and be caretaker over it.

Kent Keller

46
The NeverEnding Story

- PG
- 94 minutes
- A 1984 adaptation of the novel of the same name

Synopsis and Review

After borrowing a mysterious ornately bound book, Bastian (Barrett Oliver) is drawn into a fantasy world that is being threatened by a void known as the Nothing. He must rely on the heroism of a young warrior, Atreyu (Noah Hathaway) and his own vicarious involvement.

This film is one of the most creative movies ever made. It is a tale reminiscent of C. S. Lewis's *The Chronicles of Narnia*. With a core of characters rivaled by none, it emphasizes keeping your dreams and using your imagination. Kids and adults will love this magical story. It is a spellbinding look into the wonderful world of imagination; once you get there, you will glimpse its hidden truths.

Suggestions for Viewing

It is best to see this film in its entirety. There are bits and pieces of great discussion material strewn throughout. Watch *Story* for yourself first . . . then with your kids. You won't regret it.

Story is rated PG mainly due to some dark and frightening scenes. There is no offensive language or behavior in the film.

Important Scenes and/or Quotes

In this scene, about halfway through the film, Atreyu finally faces Gamork, the evil antagonist, in a confrontation of good versus evil. We find out why Nothing is destroying Fantasia and what the movie is all about—the loss of imagination.

Atreyu:	I will not die easily. I am a brave warrior.
Gamork:	Brave warrior, then fight the Nothing.
Atreyu:	But I can't. I can't get past the boundaries of Fantasia.
Gamork:	Ha, ha, ha.
Atreyu:	What's so funny about that?
Gamork:	Fantasia has no boundaries.
Atreyu:	That's not true. You're lying.
Gamork:	Foolish boy, don't you know anything about Fantasia? It's the world of human fantasy. Every part, every piece of it is a part of the hopes and dreams of mankind. Therefore, it has no boundaries.
Atreyu:	But why is Fantasia dying then?
Gamork:	Because people have begun to lose their hope and forget their dreams, so the Nothing grows stronger.
Atreyu:	What is the Nothing?
Gamork:	It's the emptiness that's left. It's like a despair that is trying to destroy the world, and I have been trying to help it.
Atreyu:	But why?
Gamork:	Because people who have no hopes are easy to control. And whoever has the control has the power.
Atreyu:	Who are you really?
Gamork:	I am the servant of the power behind the Nothing.

Discussion Questions

What's so important about having an imagination?

What have you accomplished because of your big dreams?

How does imagination relate to success in life?

Do you agree with Gamork? Why or why not?

Why are some people not even aware that there is a problem?

Why did God make us with so many hopes and dreams?

With what does God want us to fill our minds?

Are fantasies wrong? Why or why not?

What are some spiritual nothings we must look out for?

What does God expect of us as "hope warriors?"

Outline of Talk or Wrap-up

Although this movie deals with the loss of imagination, Gamork relates a deep truth when he says, "People who have no hopes are easy to control." It is important to relate the fact that we must be aware of what we put in our minds (Phil. 4:8).

Satan can only control us if we allow him to. God wants us to fill our minds with heavenly things. The difference between God and Satan is that Satan will control us. God, on the other hand, doesn't control us, but gives us the ability to hope, to dream, and to achieve more than we could ever imagine.

Related Bible References

Romans 5:5; Romans 12:12; Hebrews 11:1; Joel 2:28; Philippians 4:8.

Other Ideas

Discussing the sheer creativity of this movie is a great starting point for discussing the creativity of God. Examine the creation and other biblical events. You will find that God seldom did things in a usual way.

Tim and Patty Atkins

47
1984

- R
- 115 minutes
- A 1985 film based on the classic novel by George Orwell

Synopsis and Review

1984 is an anti-Utopian vision of what Orwell suspected the world may become if the forces of totalitarianism gain the upper hand. It is the story of Winston Smith (John Hurt) who works for the Ministry of Truth, a division of INGSOC, the governing party of the country Oceania. Winston is responsible for recording and rewriting history. INGSOC controls every aspect of a person's life with ubiquitous two-way telescreens that continuously broadcast government propaganda and display Big Brother's image.

Winston becomes disillusioned by the government's effort to control people by limiting their vocabulary. The Party is attempting to reduce the total number of words in "Newspeak," the official language of Oceania. As part of his private rebellion, Winston keeps a secret journal where he records the events of his life and his reflections on "truth." He also becomes interested in the underground Resistance movement. By chance he meets Julia (Susan Hamilton), who is also disenchanted with the omnipresent control of Big Brother. Winston and Julia develop a relationship. They set up numerous secret rendezvous to engage in sex, an act strongly discouraged by the government's Anti-Sex league. Eventually, they declare their mutual love for one another.

Winston also meets O'Brien (Richard Burton), who secretly gives him a copy of a book, *The Theory And Practice Of Oligarchical Collectivism* concealed within the pages of a

Newspeak dictionary. This book is attributed to the leader of the underground resistance movement—Goldstein. It reveals the manipulative principles by which Oceania is governed. O'Brien, however, works for the Party (he even claims to have written Goldstein's book), and Winston and Julia are eventually arrested. In the end, they are forced to confess their crimes. More important, they are tortured into renouncing their love for each other while pledging their love to Big Brother.

Suggestions for Viewing

Seen in its entirety *1984* is a potent movie with a powerful message. However, this movie does contain some potentially offensive material. Several nude scenes are scattered throughout the film. In addition, the torture scenes leading up to Winston's confession are graphic. Definitely preview this film before showing it to your group. Considering the above, you may want to use selected clips and quotes from the film with an explanation of the story line. See the suggestions below.

Important Scenes and/or Quotes

The movie opens with the quotation: "Who controls the past controls the future. Who controls the present controls the past." This is the central theme of the film. *1984* is about controlling people through surveillance and thought control. The following illustrate the importance of this point:

1. The scenes throughout the beginning of the movie that picture large audiences, yelling and screaming, and being manipulated through mass hysteria.
2. The various scenes throughout the film of Winston rewriting history. Winston reflects on his work: "Everything fades into mist. The past is erased. Lie becomes truth, then becomes a lie again."
3. The INGSOC Party propaganda: "War is peace. Freedom is slavery. Ignorance is strength." This is continuously broadcast on the telescreens.
4. The scene where Winston goes to O'Brien's office, and O'Brien is able to turn off his telescreen. The ability to control one's environment versus being controlled is

revealing. His explanation of the resistance movement and collective activity versus individual acts is
provocative.
5. Winston's words to Julia: "It's not so much staying alive,
but staying human. What's important is not betraying
one another; not confessing, but stopping loving one
another. The one thing they can't do is make you
believe it. They can't get to your heart." This reveals the
necessity of changing people on the inside, not just the
outside.

Discussion Questions

How does Big Brother try to limit a person's ability to think?
What role does vocabulary play in the thinking process?

What motivates people to do what they do in life?

How does God motivate people? Does he use fear or love ?

Which is a more powerful motivation: fear or love? Why?

Which is better: (1) insuring that people choose to do right by
limiting their freedom to choose; or (2) allowing people to
choose freely even when that means they choose to do
wrong? Why?

Big Brother uses lies to control people (i.e., "War is peace").
What is the relationship between lies and slavery or truth
and freedom?

Outline of Talk or Wrap-up

Use the above scenes and quotes with the Bible references
below to contrast Big Brother's god-like control over people with
how God deals with humanity. Big Brother gains people's loyalty through fear, coercion, and lies. God wins the loyalty of
men and women through love, freedom, and truth. Rather than
externally controlling people, God allows a great deal of lati-
tude—people can choose to (or not to) love and obey him. From
the beginning, God gave mankind the choice (Gen. 2:15–17).
Force leads to resentment and passive cooperation—it dehu-
manizes. Freedom embraces that which makes people human
—the ability to choose.

Related Bible References

John 8:32 (the relationship between truth and freedom); 1 John 4:18 (the relationship between fear and love); Genesis 2:15–17 (freedom as an essential human quality); and 2 Corinthians 3:17; Galatians 5:1 (on freedom in Christ).

Robert Eugene DiPaolo

48

An Officer and a Gentleman

- R
- 126 minutes
- A 1982 film

Synopsis and Review

Officer is the story of a young man breaking down the walls he has built around him, revealing who he really is. Zack Mayo (Richard Gere) has enlisted in the Navy and is at Port Ranier's Naval Aviation Officers Candidate School. He is hard-core and does not appear to care whether or not he is successful. The movie follows him through the training, focusing on his relationship with his drill sergeant, Emil Foley (Louis Gossett, Jr.), his girlfriend, Paula Pokrifki (Debra Winger), and a fellow candidate, Sid Worley (David Keith).

This film is thoroughly secular, but it draws an intense portrait of a man struggling to maintain his defensive walls. Although *Officer* contains much offensive language and several adult situations, it still is worthy in its goal to show that human beings cannot "go it alone."

Suggestions for Viewing

This movie is a good example of what it takes to build a leadership team. Zack Mayo is a powerful portrayal of a rebel and a reluctant leader who learns the value of having people work with him. The pivotal scene is the eventual breaking of his will by his drill sergeant. Through sheer physical punishment and insightful probing, the sarge takes Zack apart and shows him the real reason he is there.

Officer earns its R rating with the offensive language and adult situations referred to previously.

Important Scenes and/or Quotes

Zack wants to be an officer. But the drill sergeant believes that he is not officer material and has asked Zack to quit. When Zack refuses, Sergeant Foley decides to show Zack why he doesn't deserve to be an officer. He puts Zack through two days of physical drills, all the while probing his motives. Foley questions Zack's background, his motives, and his character.

Sarge: Give me 6 to 90. Mayo, why don't we quit this little cha-rade of yours over a couple of beers at T.J.'s. Come on, man, you are about as close to officer material as a native.

Zack: Sir, this candidate believes he would make a good officer.

Sarge: No way. No way. You don't give a——about anybody but yourself. And every one of your classmates knows it. You think they'd trust you behind the controls of a plane they have to fly in? Come on man, you're the kind who would zip off one day in my F-14 and sell it to the Cubans.

Zack: No sir. No sir. I love my country.

Sarge: Sell it to the Air Force. Talk to me. Why would a slick little hustler like you sign up for this abuse?

Zack: I want to fly jets, sir.

Sarge: My grandmother wants to fly jets.

Zack: I've wanted it ever since I was a kid.

Sarge: We're not talking about flying, we're talking about character.

Zack: I've changed. I've changed since I've been here.

Sarge: The——you have.

Zack: I've changed, sir.

Sarge: Awww. You've just polished up your act a little bit. You just shined it up. Now tell me what I want to hear. I want your DOR.

Zack: No sir.

Sarge: Your DOR.

Zack: I ain't gonna quit.

Sarge: Spell it, D-O-R. Then you can be free and get drunk with your Daddy . . .

Zack: No, sir.

Sarge: DOR.
Zack: I ain't gonna quit.
Sarge: Then you're finished. You're out.
Zack: Don't you do it. Don't you do it. I got nowhere else to go. I
got nothing else to do. Nothing else.

At this admission, the Sarge stops and then allows Zack to
continue training.

Discussion Questions

Why is it hard to admit our needs to others?
Why are we so careful not to give in and admit when we are
wrong?
What was the last confrontation that you had?
What causes people to be stubborn?
What are some things that help us see our real selves?
How does God feel about our past?
How does God help us deal with our inner pain?
How can we help other people break down their walls?

Outline of Talk or Wrap-up

Although this movie is graphic and offensive at times, this
scene shows a man in pain over who he is and also how hard it
is for the walls to come down. Explain that all of us have walls
to hide the things about ourselves that we fear. Jesus said, "You
will know the truth, and the truth will set you free" (John 8:32).
Only with God's help can we free ourselves from our fears.
Then, with the walls down we will be free to grow.

Stress that, as Christians, we are called to help others break
down their walls and open up to Christ, the Truth. When we follow Jesus' example of acceptance, compassion, and sincere
love, we allow people to be themselves without fear. We need to
show God's love to people hiding behind walls of fear and pain.

Related Bible References

John 8:32; 2 Corinthians 5:17; Psalm 139; Romans 12:2;
John 14:6.

Tim and Patty Atkins

49
On Golden Pond

- PG
- 109 minutes
- A 1981 film

Synopsis and Review

On Golden Pond takes a look at family relationships as well as relationships between the elderly and teenagers. What happens when an eighty-year-old man, preoccupied with death, and his wife, spend a month at their summer home on Golden Pond with a thirteen-year-old boy from California, whose fun activities include cruising chicks and sucking face?

The results are heartwarming as the old man, Norman Thayer, Jr. (Henry Fonda), rediscovers that life still has purpose. The thirteen-year-old, Billy (Doug McKeon), learns that there's a lot you can learn from the elderly. Through it all, Norman's wife, Ethel (Katharine Hepburn), holds the family together with her care and understanding.

Another important part of the story is the relationship between Norman and his daughter, Chelsea (Jane Fonda). They are constantly bickering. Chelsea is visiting her parents with her boyfriend (Dabney Coleman) and his son, Billy.

The movie has a happy ending as the gap between generations is closed and relationships within the family are healed.

Suggestions for Viewing

Divide the film into three sections. Section 1 is where Norman and Billy are alone for the first time.

Section 2 shows their relationship beginning to take shape. The scene begins with Billy cleaning the fish they just caught and ends with Ethel's talk with Billy.

Section 3 shows Norman and Billy going into Purgatory Cove to look for Walter, the biggest trout in the lake. It ends with Ethel finding them after their boating accident.

Warning: This PG rated movie does have offensive language so be sure to screen it first.

Important Scenes and/or Quotes

Norman and Billy live in two different worlds. This is obvious when Norman responds to Billy's comment about "sucking face" with girls, with "go and read *Treasure Island*."

After Norman accidentally sets the house on fire and yells at Billy, Ethel talks with Billy.

> He's not yelling at you, he's yelling at life. He's like an old lion, he has to remind himself that he can still roar. Sometimes you have to look hard at a person and remember that he's doing the best he can. He's just trying to find his way, that's all. Just like you.

Discussion Questions

Set up for Section 1. Say something like: "*On Golden Pond* is a story about an elderly couple, Norman and Ethel Thayer, and their life on Golden Pond, their summer home for forty years. The Thayers have one daughter, Chelsea, who lives in California. Our story picks up as Chelsea comes home for her dad's eightieth birthday party. She brings along her boyfriend and his thirteen-year-old son."

After seeing that section ask:

What do you think of first when you think of elderly people?
What has your contact with elderly people been? Was it similar to Billy's?

Set up for Section 2. Say something like: "Chelsea and her boyfriend are leaving for a month to tour Europe. They think that Europe would be boring for Billy, so Chelsea asks her parents to watch him while they're gone. Coming from a broken home, Billy is used to being shipped off, but he doesn't like being left with the 'Old Poop' and his wife. Billy discovers, however, that life with Norman and Ethel isn't that bad. He even enjoys fishing with Norman."

Afterward ask:

> After Norman yells at Billy for making such a mess putting out the fire, Ethel goes to Billy and says: "He's just trying to find his way, that's all. Just like you." What does that statement mean?
> How was Norman trying to find his way?
> How was Billy trying to find his way?
> How are you trying to find your way?

Set up for Section 3. Say something like: "Billy and Norman are good buddies by this time. They've been trying to catch Walter, a twelve-pound trout. The only place they haven't tried is Purgatory Cove, a dangerous, rock-filled section of the lake."

Afterward ask:

> What difference did Billy make in Norman's life?
> What difference did Norman make in Billy's life?
> In what ways might an elderly person be able to help you?
> What might you learn from an older person?
> In what ways might you be able to help an elderly person?

Outline of Talk or Wrap-up

Explain to students that we need to respect the elderly, not make fun of them because of the way they drive or the stories they tell for the fifth time. We need to understand the experience an elderly person has and the wisdom they can pass on. We need to see what we can learn from someone who's been "through the fire," who's trusted God through thick and thin.

It is also important to realize that we can make a difference in an elderly person's life. The time we spend with an elderly person really brightens his or her day.

The Lord calls each of us to serve, and that includes serving the elderly. Encourage students to think of key ways that they can serve them.

Encourage students to see that they can be an example to the elderly. First Timothy 4:12 says, "Don't let anyone think little of you because you are young. Be their ideal; let them follow the way you teach and live; be a pattern for them in your love, your faith, and your clean thoughts" (LB). You have much to offer an elderly person.

Related Bible References

Proverbs 20:29; Galatians 5:13; 2 Kings 2:23; 1 Timothy 4:12.

Other Ideas

On Golden Pond could also be used to discuss relationships between parents and their children, especially the role between fathers and daughters. You could also use the film to discuss the issue of death and dying.

Janet Wielenga and Trent Bushnell

50
One Flew Over the Cuckoo's Nest

- R
- 129 minutes
- A 1975 film

Synopsis and Review

Jack Nicholson plays Randle Patrick McMurphy, a prison inmate who gets himself transferred to a mental hospital by acting crazy. There he is placed under the direct care of Nurse Mildred Ratched (Louise Fletcher), a manipulative and controlling nurse. McMurphy creates havoc by continually bucking the system and instilling an independent spirit in the usually stoic patients.

This movie won a number of Oscars including Best Picture. It is a gritty look at our care of the mentally ill a number of years ago. Jack Nicholson gives a fine performance as a man concerned only for his own well-being until he realizes the injustice of the system.

Suggestions for Viewing

Cuckoo's Nest presents a great example of the impact that one man can have on others. It would be best to show several scenes where McMurphy challenges the standard and likewise encourages his fellow patients to do the same thing.

Warnings: *Cuckoo's Nest* is rated R because of the profane language and adult situations, including an attempted suicide.

Important Scenes and/or Quotes

There's a storm brewing between McMurphy and Nurse Ratched over the control of the eleven other patients in the therapy group. After asking for a change in the schedule so they can watch the World Series, McMurphy is told that changes are made only with the consensus of the group. When the other members of the group are too afraid to challenge Nurse Ratched, the schedule stays as it is. McMurphy is so frustrated by this and the passivity of his friends, that he tells them he is going to go in the bathroom, rip the sink out of the floor and toss it through the window so he can go downtown to watch the Series. All the patients gather around to watch him. They are amazed at what he is doing . . . that he would try to buck authority by doing the impossible. When he fails, he turns to the group and says, "At least I tried. At least I tried."

McMurphy's action inspires the other patients, so they ask Nurse Ratched for another vote. This time they all vote in favor of the schedule change, but are still denied it on the basis of a technicality. Not to be thwarted, McMurphy sits in front of the television screen and calls an imaginary game. His enthusiasm is so overwhelming that the other patients gather around and cheer imaginary runs and hits. Nurse Ratched sits and watches the group, knowing that for now she cannot break their unity.

Discussion Questions

What kind of person does Randle McMurphy remind you of? How about Nurse Ratched?

Why do they have a problem with each other?

Why do we enjoy people like McMurphy so much?

Why do we find people like Nurse Ratched less desirable?

When is it helpful to have someone like Nurse Ratched around?

What kind of Christian would McMurphy be? How about Nurse Ratched?

When is God like McMurphy? When is he like Nurse Ratched?

Using Nurse Ratched as one extreme and McMurphy as the other, describe how we should be as Christians.

What did McMurphy risk by his actions?

What did he accomplish?

What kind of risks does God want us to take as Christians?

Outline of Talk or Wrap-up

Begin by talking about people who have taken risks and thus have changed the world—for example, Martin Luther King, Jr., the apostle Paul, Mother Teresa, and others. Point out that their bravery and creativity were shown as they changed what had previously been a standard. Point out that most people who have made lasting changes have had the touch of God in what they did. Remind them that the whole plan of God is against what the world views as standard.

Explain that God wants Christians to be the risk takers who change those around them. We need to take advantage of the opportunities around us and create a new and different world. Acknowledge that there is fear in taking risks. God is aware of that. He can handle that fear if we are willing to take the risk and try. There is nothing wrong with failing. As McMurphy would say, "At least you tried. At least you tried."

Related Bible References

1 Samuel 23:16; 1 Thessalonians 5:11; Hebrews 3:13; 1 Timothy 2:2.

Tim and Patty Atkins

51
Ordinary People

- R
- 123 minutes
- A 1980 film based on the novel by Judith Guest

Synopsis and Review

This dramatic film, which won four Academy Awards including the Oscar for Best Picture, chronicles the disintegration of the Jarrett family after its eldest son, Bucky, drowns in a boating accident.

Timothy Hutton stars as Conrad, the guilt-ridden younger son who survived the accident and feels personally responsible for his brother's death. Not only has Conrad withdrawn from family and friends, but he has also attempted suicide.

Mary Tyler Moore plays Conrad's mother, Beth, a cold, aloof, self-centered woman who cares more about how things look to others than she does about looking honestly at her own life and at her relationships.

Donald Sutherland is Calvin, Conrad's desperately confused father who is unable to understand either his wife or his son, and who, despite his best efforts, cannot seem to bring them together.

In the end, Conrad and his father begin to find emotional healing through each other and through a competent counselor named Berger (played by Judd Hirsch). Beth, however, threatened by the thought of having to work through her problems and grief, packs her bags and leaves.

Suggestions for Viewing

Despite the strong language that permeates this movie,

there are several profanity-free scenes that capture the empti-
ness of the Jarrett family, the superficiality of their relationships,
and their extreme pain.

- The first few minutes of the film give us a glimpse of the
  sterility of the Jarrett home. Despite the appearance of
  order (everything is in its place) we quickly realize that this
  family is in a state of emotional chaos.
- The scene in which Conrad catches his mom reminiscing in
  the deceased brother's bedroom is painful to watch as
  mother and son awkwardly attempt to connect. They never
  do.
- The party scene (attended by Calvin and Beth) is filled with
  empty small talk and perfectly conveys the shallowness of
  the Jarrett's social circle.
- The scene after choir practice illustrates the power of an
  encouraging word. Pratt (Elizabeth McGovern) praises
  Conrad's singing voice, and, in one of the few humorous
  moments of the film, Conrad sings in a booming voice all
  the way home.

This movie is filled with scenes that will touch a chord
among your young people. Preview it, pick out one or two of
the above scenes (or any of its other powerful moments), ask
some probing questions, and watch kids open up.

Why is this film such an excellent discussion starter?
Because more and more in our culture, people (especially adolescents) feel alienated. They long for deep, intimate, satisfying
relationships.

Warning: Despite an excellent script, brilliant direction
(Robert Redford won an Oscar), and first rate acting, *Ordinary
People* is a thoroughly depressing movie.

The Jarretts are alienated individuals who do not know how
to communicate without yelling, clamming up, or using
extreme profanity; moreover, they are a family which does not
recognize the emotional healing that is available in Jesus
Christ.

And the most sobering realization of all? This family, with
all its problems, is the rule rather than the exception. Indeed,
the Jarretts are "ordinary people."

Important Scenes and/or Quotes

1. Beth tries to numb the pain in her life through vacations, shopping, and dinner parties. While eating dinner at the mall, her husband suggests family counseling. Beth's obsession with how things look and her stubborn reluctance to acknowledge or deal with the problems in her life are clearly seen:

   I don't want to see any doctors or counselors. I'm me. This is *my* family. And if we have problems we will solve them in the privacy of our own home. Not by running to some kind of specialist every time something goes wrong.

2. Another telling remark comes from Conrad in the context of a counseling session. His therapist asks, "Is any place easy?" Conrad replies, "The hospital was." "It was? Why?" "Because nobody hid anything there."

   The clear implication is that relationships are simplified (and more rewarding) when the participants are committed to honesty and openness.

Discussion Questions

Why do you think this movie is called *Ordinary People*?

Why is it so hard for many teenagers to talk openly, honestly, and civilly with their parents?

This movie suggests that Mrs. Jarrett enjoyed her older son, Bucky, more than she liked Conrad. Put yourself in Conrad's place. How do you feel?

What do you think was going on inside Mrs. Jarrett that caused her to act as she did?

How do most people respond to tragic situations? How do *you* think you would react if you lost a brother or sister in a drowning accident?

Where is God in this movie?

Suppose Conrad Jarrett was a classmate and friend of yours. What could you say to him? How might you help him through his pain?

Outline of Talk or Wrap-up

Option # 1: Dealing With Death

1. *Death—a fact of life.* Death may come suddenly or not for a long time, but it *will* come.
2. *Grief—that bad feeling that's good for you.* Grief is a necessary part of emotional healing; however, many people, like the characters in the movie, try to avoid the grief process through various means:

   A. Temporary escapes (vacationing, shopping, over-involvement at school or work, chemical abuse, sex, television, movies)
   B. Permanent escape (suicide)
   C. Denial (insistence that "I'm strong. I'm okay. Big boys—and girls—don't cry.")

3. *Hope—what we find in the Author of Life and Conqueror of Death.* Apart from Christ, there is no ultimate hope. It is good that Conrad finally understands the need to forgive himself, but he also needs to experience God's forgiveness.

Option #2: Relationships

1. Life is composed of relationships (with parents, siblings, friends, classmates, coaches, etc.) Which relationships matter most to you?
2. Even in *ideal* circumstances, good relationships take hard work. Why is it so difficult to communicate and get along with others?
3. Tough times will destroy shallow relationships. How will *your* relationships hold up when trials come?
4. The "vertical" affects the "horizontal." Do you have that one relationship (i.e. a personal relationship with God through Christ) that can not only help you love others but also see you through life's tough times?

Related Bible References

1 Corinthians 15 is perfect for discussions on death. For lessons on dealing with life's difficulties, see 2 Corinthians 4:8–18. In discussing the alienation that we feel in our relation-

Video Movies Worth Watching

ships, as well as our tendencies to hide from and hurt (i.e. blame) each other, there is no better passage than Genesis 3:1–13. Ephesians 2:1–10 describes the hopeless and helpless situation of people who do not know God and what Christ has done to save them. Verses 11–22 further discuss how Christ breaks down barriers that separate individuals.

Other Ideas

Use scenes from *Ordinary People* to launch discussions about suicide, encouragement, friendship, or communication.

Len Woods

52
The Outsiders

- PG
- 91 minutes
- A 1983 film based on the book by S.E. Hinton

Synopsis and Review

It would be possible to get young people to watch this movie by simply asking if they would like to see a film starring Swayze, Cruise, Lowe, Dillon, Estevez, and Macchio. The cast is almost a "who's who" of stars.

The setting for *The Outsiders* is Tulsa, Oklahoma, circa 1966. The main types of kids in town are the "socs" (pronounced soshs—athletes, cheerleaders, etc.), and the "greasers" (dropouts, hoods, etc.). These two social groups are constantly in conflict with each other. Several people on each side realize that there is no winning and no meaning in the battles, but the fighting goes on. One of the young greasers (Ralph Macchio) kills a drunk soc in self-defense and is accompanied by a friend, Dallas (Matt Dillon), in his escape. While hiding from the law, they end up rescuing several children from a burning building and become heroes. In the process, however, the greaser is burned badly and ultimately dies. Dallas, who has related with his young friends all along has a difficult time seeing why they should care for anyone outside their group. He can't understand that anyone other than another greaser is worth helping. The death of the young boy sends him over the edge, and he dies in a hail of police gunfire.

The film ends with a note being read that the burned greaser had written before his death. He encourages his friend Ponyboy to "stay gold"; to see the goodness in life.

This film gives a haunting look at life reduced to tribal

loyalties without any spiritual values. The only rules become (a) always be loyal to your group, and (b) always fight fair. There is little real hope in this story.

Suggestions for Viewing

There is some profanity although it is toned down. To get the film's full effect, it should be viewed in its entirety.

Important Scenes and/or Quotes

1. The lyrics of the credit song "Stay Gold" by Stevie Wonder state the underlying theme of the film.
2. The scene of Ponyboy's quoting a Robert Frost poem and his friend's reaction is worth seeing twice.

Discussion Questions

What groups in your school relate to each other in ways similar to the socs and the greasers?

How real were the attitudes and conversations in the movie?

Which character in this movie do you think you are most like?

Who is the hero in this film? Who is the bad guy?

Who seems to understand what is going on in the town?

How would you describe Dallas's view of life?

What do you think it means to stay gold?

If Jesus used this film as one of his parables, what lessons might he try to teach?

Outline of Talk or Wrap-up

Say something like: "When I watch this movie I wonder if anyone can really stay gold. Have you ever met someone who stayed gold; who never lost the newness, the love for living that the people in this movie are looking for? I think the truth is that the movie reaches out to us because most of us realize we haven't stayed gold. When we finally notice a rainbow, a sunset, or something truly beautiful, what we feel is a kind of deep longing for something we've lost along the way. Or maybe we never had anything but the desire in the first place.

"So what can we do with a life in which we've already lost the gold, or never had it? *First,* we have to realize how much that last sentence and this film describes basic human nature. The Bible puts it this way: 'All have sinned and fall short of the glory of God.' I'd call that missing the gold.

"*Second,* we need to realize that if the gold, the newness, and cleanness is missing, the only way we'll have it is to receive it from someone as a gift. Listen to this: 'When someone becomes a Christian he becomes a brand new person inside. He is not the same any more. A new life has begun!' (2 Cor. 5:17, LB). The message of the gospel isn't stay gold; the message of the gospel is that in Jesus Christ we can become gold."

(Note: Develop this parallel of eternal life being gold and invite students to consider accepting God's gift.)

Related Bible References

1 Peter 1:4–7 (God has reserved the priceless gift of eternal life for his children; your faith is more precious to God than gold.)

Neil Wilson

53
Papillon

- PG
- 153 minutes
- A 1973 film based on the true story of Henri "Papillon" Charriere

Synopsis and Review

Papillon recounts one man's struggle for freedom. Papillon (Steve McQueen), a Frenchman, is accused of murder and, though he claims to be innocent, is sent to French Guyana as a prisoner for the duration of his life.

Papillon refuses to accept his sentence and plots his escape. After one failed attempt, he is sentenced to two years in solitary confinement of which six months are in total darkness. Though he borders on insanity during the long months, he finds ways to maintain his mental sharpness.

After those two years, he plans another breakout, this time with two friends. They are caught when the threesome finally reaches the mainland of South America, but Papillon evades the police until some nuns from a convent turn him in.

He is sentenced to five more years in solitary confinement and then sent to an island to die. Escape seems impossible (to get to the water he would have to jump from a cliff) and all of the other inmates resign themselves to that fact. Not Papillon. He stuffs coconuts in an old burlap bag, throws it into the water, and plunges in after it.

Papillon reaches the mainland and is never caught.

Suggestions for Viewing

No one scene in *Papillon* stands out. They all fit together, so you may want to view it in its entirety. An edited version, however, would be possible. There is some rough language and also some nudity, so preview the film before showing it to a group.

Important Scenes and/or Quotes

Louis Degas (Dustin Hoffman) talks to Papillon on his release from solitary confinement. Degas offers to get Papillon an easy job around the hospital and thinks his lawyers have found a way to gain his release within three years. Papillon responds that three years is too long.

> **Degas:** Tell me what you want.
> **Papillon:** A boat.
> **Degas:** I should have known.

On the island, Papillon contemplates freedom. Degas is there too. Together they stand on a cliff overlooking the water.

> **Papillon:** The mainland is only twenty-four miles away. You just float with the current.
> **Degas:** That seems so desperate.
> **Papillon:** Yea.
> **Degas:** Think it will work?
> **Papillon:** Does it matter?

Discussion Questions

Why was Papillon so desirous of freedom? How much did Degas want his freedom? Whom are you more like?

How would you define freedom?

What type of freedom does Jesus offer? Could it be argued that without Jesus no one can really be free?

How can people be enslaved even though they aren't in prison? How can people who are in prison still be free?

If a person has a relationship with Jesus and is free, how should his or her life be different?

In what ways are you free? What could you do to live that freedom more fully?

Outline of Talk or Wrap-up

Use *Papillon* as a way to discuss freedom.

Explain that prisoner Papillon is an example of many people. They want to be free and will go to any extent in their search for freedom. Others, like Degas, want to be free but are not willing to pay the price for that freedom.

Explain the freedom that is ours in Christ. Though others will say that their struggle for freedom has no religious ties, make it clear that God alone offers substantial freedom. Only forgiveness through Jesus can offer the freedom that people desire. Freedom that does not include the forgiveness is not true freedom.

Encourage each person to examine their relationship to Christ. Make it clear that those who do stand in relationship with him are free (and should be living that way) and those who do not have such a relationship are kidding themselves if they think they are free.

Offer them the chance to meet Jesus.

Related Bible References

Romans 7:14–20 (slaves to sin); Psalm 118:5 (freedom comes from God); John 8 (freedom through the Son); Romans 6 (freedom from sin).

Other Ideas

Papillon would also be useful in a discussion about friendship, using the bond between Degas and Papillon as a powerful example. The film could also be helpful in raising questions about the government's role in punishment.

Jared Reed

54

Parenthood

- PG-13
- 124 minutes
- A 1989 film

Synopsis and Review

Parenthood presents a stark picture of the trials and joys of parenting. While good for laughs, this movie also touches on a long list of parent-child issues in a realistic and hard-hitting manner.

Parenthood is the story of Gil Buckman (Steve Martin) and his entire extended family—at its worst. Key segments deal with teen sex, pornography, masturbation, illegitimate children, separation, authority, and divorce. Positive interactions don't really develop until the end, when virtually every member of the family begins to see his or her mistakes and blossoms into a mature, insightful family member. As contrived as the "one big happy family" ending is, it lends real hope to families facing problems.

Suggestions for Viewing

Parenthood is good for raising issues and questions, rather than for providing answers. As a discussion starter, therefore, the movie certainly could be shown in its entirety. An endless discussion could follow, listing the issues, discussing the movie's perspective, and adding a Christian perspective.

A second option would be a condensed version with the scenes described below.

Warning: *Parenthood* contains occasional swearing and deals with some sensitive issues.

Important Scenes and/or Quotes

1. Five minutes into the movie, Garry (Leaf Phoenix) walks out on his mother, Helen (Dianne Wiest). The issue to discuss here is parent/teen communication.

2. At twelve minutes, the precocious child, Patty (Ivyann Schwan), recites for her parents, Nathan (Rick Moranis) and Susan (Harley Kozak), who are pressuring her intellectually at a very early age. The focus of this scene is high parental expectations.

3. At the one-hour mark, Garry's divorced dad refuses to allow Garry to move in with him. The topic here could be the effects of divorce on the children involved.

4. One hour and five minutes into *Parenthood*, there is an elaborate birthday party hosted by Gil and his wife for their son. This illustrates the extreme actions parents will often take to please their children.

5. In a scene at one hour and thirty-eight minutes, Gil quits his job because it interferes with his family. This would be a good starter for a discussion on family tensions or personal values.

6. Perhaps the strongest scene to illustrate what it takes to be a parent—they hope for the best while fearing the worst—occurs fifty-five minutes into the movie. Gil is coaching Kevin's baseball team. As the opponents send a batter up in the last inning with the winning run on base, Gil daydreams about Kevin speaking at his high school graduation. He fades back to reality at the sound of the bat and watches in slow motion as Kevin drops a pop-up and loses the game. Then Gil daydreams about Kevin shooting a gun from a tower. Gil tells the police, "I did the best I could" (as a father).

Follow that scene with one at one hour and forty-five minutes into the movie where Kevin catches a fly ball to win the game, and Gil goes crazy.

Discussion Questions

In what ways do your parents show that they hope for the best for you?

Frank Buckman (Jason Robards, left) and his son Gil (Steve Martin, right) discuss their distant relationship.

Gil Buckman (Steve Martin, right) offers advice and encouragement to his son Kevin (Jasen Fisher, left).

In what ways do they sometimes show that they fear the worst? (curfew, questions about friends, over-protect, etc.)

What could you do to alleviate their fears and make it easier for them to trust you?

Outline of Talk or Wrap-up

Parents are new to parenting, just as you are new to growing up.

If your parents really want what's best for you, and want you to avoid the consequences of bad choices, they need you to help them succeed.

As you struggle for your independence, try to figure out what they're trying to do with their many unexplainable actions. Don't alienate the people who care about you the most!

First Corinthians 13:4–7 says: "Love is very patient and kind, never jealous or envious, never boastful or proud, never haughty or selfish or rude. Love does not demand its own way. It is not irritable or touchy. It does not hold grudges and will hardly even notice when others do it wrong. It is never glad about injustice, but rejoices whenever truth wins out. If you love someone you will be loyal to him no matter what the cost. You will always believe in him, always expect the best of him, and always stand your ground in defending him" (LB).

If you love your parents in this way, it will make it easier for them to do the same. And in most cases, that's exactly what you both want.

Related Bible References

1 Timothy 4:12 (set an example); Philippians 2:3–4 (don't be selfish, be interested in others); Ephesians 6:1–4 (parents and children each have an important role to play in the family).

Trent Bushnell and Janet Wielenga

55
A Place in the Sun

- Unrated
- 122 minutes
- A 1951 black and white classic based on the novel, *An American Tragedy*, by Theodore Dreiser

Synopsis and Review

A Place in the Sun stars Montgomery Clift as George Eastman, a young man heading out to escape his past and to make it on his own. Leaving behind a life of poverty and the religious mission work of his parents, George finds employment with his rich uncle, Charles Eastman (Herbert Heyes), a president of the Eastman swimsuit company. Eventually George is able to move his way up in the company as well as into the social circle of the Eastman family and Angela Vickers (the girl of his dreams played by Elizabeth Taylor). On the way up, however, he meets Alice Trip (Shelly Winters), an assembly line worker at the Eastman company. Out of lonely desperation George violates the company policy against dating employees and becomes romantically involved with Alice.

As fate would have it, the same night (his birthday) he finally meets Angela, Alice tells him she's pregnant. What follows is an internal battle between obligation and opportunity; desperation and desire. Alice becomes more demanding as Angela becomes more delightful. Alice insists that George marry her; Angela informs George that she loves him and intends to marry him. George is caught between paying the consequences for his past sins and pursuing a bright future (George's uncle informs him that he has plans for him in the company).

Frustrated and confused, George contemplates killing Alice. He goes as far as taking her out on a deserted lake with the intention of drowning her. At the moment of decision he can't go through with his plan. Unfortunately, Alice, who can't swim, stands up in the boat, causing it to capsize. She drowns while George manages to swim to shore. Desperately George attempts to retain what he has gained, but eventually he is arrested, convicted, and sentenced to death for Alice's murder. The movie ends with George on death row accepting responsibility for his actions and Angela reiterating her love for him.

Suggestions for Viewing

A Place in the Sun is worth watching in its entirety. It contains no objectionable language nor objectionable scenes. The dramatic exploration of one man's motivation to obtain security and significance and the vivid portrayal of the consequences of sin are best seen in the unraveling of the movie's plot. The progression of the film creates tension that could be used to generate thoughtful discussion. Still segments of this film could be powerfully employed with a plot summary. See suggestions below.

Important Scenes and/or Quotes

1. Early on, out of insecurity, Alice says to George, "If you're an Eastman you're not in the same boat as anyone." Later, also out of insecurity, she retracts this statement. Ironically, a picture of George, Angela, and friends in a boat tips Alice off to George's double life.
2. The pivotal contrast in scenes midway through the movie, where George goes from dancing with Angela to being told by Alice that she's pregnant, sets up the central crisis around which the rest of the movie revolves.
3. The inception and development of the temptation to murder Alice are revealing. It begins with George reluctantly marking Sept. 1 on his calendar, the date Alice has demanded they get married. He hears a news report about accidents and drowning. The seed is planted. The seed is watered when Angela mentions the drowning of a couple last year on Loon Lake.

4. In George's defense, his lawyer points out that there is a difference between thought and deed, desire and action. George finds himself wrestling with this as he awaits execution. This comes to fruition when his mother and a minister visit him in prison. The minister makes the point that people often hide the truth from themselves. He asks George, "When you were on the lake and the boat capsized, at that moment when you might have saved her (Alice), who were you thinking of, Alice or another girl?" George sees Angela's face. The minister sees it in his eyes and tells him, "In your heart was murder, George." George admits his guilt to Angela when she comes to see him, "I know something now I didn't know before. I'm guilty of a lot of the things, most of what they say."

Discussion Questions

For whom do you have the most compassion: Alice, Angela, or George? Explain your answer.

Did George ever love Alice, or was he merely trying to cure his loneliness?

Did Alice love George, or was she merely trying to gain some sense of security for herself? Did she want her place in the sun as much as George did? If she really loved him should she have let him go?

Did George love Angela or merely the idea of having someone like Angela love and accept him?

What really motivated George: (1) fear; (2) true love; (3) desire to get ahead; or (4) desire to escape his past?

Was George guilty of murdering Alice? Why or why not? Why did George finally conclude that he was guilty? Do you agree with him?

Outline of Talk or Wrap-up

A lesson could be introduced by or built around the following themes that emerge from A Place in the Sun—finding security and significance in life; the evolution and fruition of temptation; the consequences of sin; and the internal origin of outward behavior (sin). George tries to find security and significance in his relationship with Angela and the potential of upward mobility in his Uncle's company. The temptation of killing Alice is followed from its inception to its realization. The point that sin's origin is man's inward corruption is made plain as George comes to the realization that he is guilty of killing Alice.

Related Bible References

Matthew 5:21–48 (guilt from the internal intention, not just the external action); Genesis 3:6 (a description of the evolution and fruition of temptation); Proverbs 1:31 (the consequences of sin); and Proverbs 2:11 (the necessity of discretion and understanding).

Robert Eugene DiPaolo

56
Places in the Heart

- PG
- 113 minutes
- A 1984 film

Synopsis and Review

Set in Waxahachie, Texas in 1935 (during the Depression), *Places in the Heart* is the story of Mrs. Edna Spalding (Sally Field). Her husband, Royce Spalding, is accidentally killed by a drunk black man named Wylie. Left with little money and a substantial mortgage on their home, Edna and her children, Frank (Yankton Hatten), and Possum (Gennie James) are forced to make ends meet on their own.

Along the way, the Spaldings take in two tenants. First, there's Moze (Danny Glover), a black man looking for work, food, and a place to stay. After overcoming her initial reservations, Mrs. Spalding agrees to let Moze stay on to help grow cotton. She has concluded that growing cotton is the only way she can earn the money to pay the mortgage. She also reluctantly agrees to take in Mr. Will (John Malkovich), the brother-in-law of Mr. Demby (Lane Smith), the banker. Mr. Will, who is blind, supports himself by weaving cane chairs and brooms.

At harvest, Mrs. Spalding is faced with a drop in the price of cotton. She decides to risk hiring extra cotton pickers so that she can bring in the first crop of cotton and win a much needed extra $100. Surviving a sweltering harvest, night and day picking, and shrewd price negotiations, Mrs. Spalding not only brings in the season's first crop but she also gets the price she needs to meet her financial obligations.

Places also weaves into the movie a sub-story about

221

Edna's sister, Margaret (Lindsay Crouse), and her husband, Wayne (Ed Harris). While Mrs. Spalding symbolizes dignity and strength, Wayne represents depravity and weakness. He is involved in an affair with Viola (Amy Madigan). And it is only after Viola decides to end their relationship, convincing her husband, Buddy, (Terry O'Quinn) to move to Houston, that Wayne repents and seeks reconciliation with his wife.

Suggestions for Viewing

Places contains nothing that would be considered questionable or offensive. While you could use any of the powerful scenes (described below) in isolation, *Places* is a movie that is best viewed in its entirety. The development of the many themes and sub-themes are best enjoyed as the movie unfolds.

Important Scenes and/or Quotes

Following are several themes and scenes that could be used as discussion starters or as part of a wrap-up talk.

1. Prejudice and racism, illustrated by: (a) The contrast between Royce's and Wylie's funerals; (b) The treatment of Moze by Margaret, Mr. Simmons the gin owner, and ultimately by the group of hooded men who beat him up.
2. Hypocrisy and manipulation, illustrated by the scenes involving Mrs. Spalding and Mr. Demby: (a) Their first encounter the day after the funeral where he tries to convince her to sell her home and land, and even to split up her family if necessary; (b) Their second encounter in the bank when Mrs. Spalding informs him of her plan to grow cotton—he tells her that she's ignorant; (c) Their third encounter when he forces her, in the name of Christian charity, to take as a border, his brother-in-law, Mr. Will.
3. Strength of character revealed in crisis, illustrated by: (a) Edna's sheer determination to keep her home, land, and family and what she does to do it; (b) Moze's courage to advise Mrs. Spalding on purchasing the cotton seed,

negotiating its selling price, and saving Frank from the tornado; (c) Mr. Will's rescue of Possum during the tornado and his rescue of Moze from his hooded assailants; (d) Frank in accepting punishment for smoking and his running home to help his family during the tornado.

4. Weakness of character revealed by crisis, illustrated by: (a) Wayne's weakness in dealing with his relationship with both Viola and his wife; (b) Viola in her running away from her problems (the affair with Wayne), rather than dealing with them; (c) Mr. Demby in his various manipulative and condescending dealings with Mrs. Spalding; (d) Mr. Simmons and the other men who hid behind hoods as they beat up Moze.

5. Love, reconciliation, and forgiveness: (a) The last surreal scene of the movie sums up this central theme. Moze, Wylie, and Royce mysteriously participate in a communion service with the rest of the main characters from the movie. (b) Margaret and Wayne are also reconciled at the above church service.

Discussion Questions

What kind of person is Mr. Demby the banker? What motivates him?

How does Mr. Demby's hiding behind the guise of Christian charity and duty make you feel? When have you used your Christian beliefs to cover other motives?

What makes people prejudiced? Why did Mr. Simmons dislike and mistreat Moze?

Describe the essential differences between the characters of Mrs. Spalding and Wayne. What motivates Edna? What motivates Wayne? With whom do you identify more, Edna or Royce?

What point is the last scene in the movie trying to make?

If you were Margaret would you have forgiven Wayne? Why is it difficult to forgive those who are the closest to us?

How did trials and hard times impact and affect Edna Spalding?

Outline of Talk or Wrap-up

Places is about determination, beating the odds, and human relationships. Use one or more of the above themes with the Scripture references below to develop, illustrate, or wrap up a talk.

Related Bible References

1 Corinthians 13:1–8 (quoted at the film's conclusion about the nature of love); Colossians 3:13 (forgiveness); Proverbs 10:12 (power of hate and love); Proverbs 4:23; 6:14; 12:25; 13:12; 16:21; and 20:5 (issues of the heart); Romans 5:3–4; James 1:2–5 (trials and perseverance as character builders); James 2:15–16 (empty words without actions); John 4:1–30 (example of Jesus overcoming Jewish prejudice against the Samaritans); and the examples of the courageous women, Ruth and Esther.

Robert Eugene DiPaolo

57
Presumed Innocent

- R
- 127 minutes
- A 1990 film based on the novel by Scott Turow

Synopsis and Review

Harrison Ford deviates from his more famous roles as Indiana Jones and Han Solo to play the part of Rusty Sabich in this film. Although Rusty is a lawyer in the county prosecutor's office, he finds himself the defendant in the murder trial of a female co-worker (with whom he had an affair). The evidence is convincing but Rusty adamantly defends his innocence. With the help of a savvy lawyer (Raul Julia) and of a loyal detective, the charges against Rusty are dropped.

Just as the turmoil seems resolved, however, Rusty discovers that the murderer is his own wife. As the movie ends, new questions are raised.

Presumed Innocent is a compelling movie. As the drama unfolds, it becomes clear that no one is innocent—not Rusty, nor his boss, nor his lawyer, nor the judge, nor the detective, nor the murder victim, nor even Rusty's wife. Only one is on trial for breaking the law, but all of them are guilty (morally, that is).

Suggestions for Viewing

Presumed Innocent deals with important themes. Unfortunately, the presentation of the subject matter (the apparent rape and murder of a young woman) and much of the language are inappropriate in any type of church setting. Some movies are just as powerful edited—not

Presumed Innocent. The ending is effective only when the rest of the film has been "experienced." An explanation of the contents of the movie (especially emphasizing the guilt of every party) rather than short clips might be the best avenue to pursue.

Important Scenes and/or Quotes

1. The movie opens with the pan of a courtroom. Harrison Ford delivers a monologue on the importance of the law. Among other things he adds, "If they [those involved in the legal system] cannot find the truth, what is our hope of justice?"

2. Rusty and his boss talk about Rusty's first day on the job.

   Boss: When you started here you thought you could make a difference.
   Rusty: Part of me still does.
   Boss: A guy as tough as you are still hanging on to the shreds of your ideals.
   Rusty: Shreds are all I got!

3. Rusty's wife confesses to killing the woman. After detailing the murder she offers, "The destroyer is destroyed. She [the murderer] feels power . . . control . . . a sense that she is guided by a force beyond herself. The suffering was over and they were saved."
   "Saved?", questions Rusty in disbelief.

Discussion Questions

What is the difference between the "law of the land" and the "law of God"? Would the characters in the movie have seen any difference?

What would be a definition for justice in *Presumed Innocent*? What would be the Bible's definition of justice?

Who was guilty in this movie according to the courts? According to God?

What does *Presumed Innocent* teach us about sin? Who are the sinners?

Are you guilty or innocent before God? Why and/or why not?

What means has God offered us to deal with our guilt? What did Jesus do? What are we supposed to do?

Outline of Talk or Wrap-up

Use the themes in *Presumed Innocent* to help teach about the universality of sin.

Stress that though a person may never be put on trial, everyone is guilty before God. Relate that God's standards are much different than the standards of a court of law. Although human standards may deviate, God continually demands perfection (not only in behavior but also in motivation and attitude). None of us is innocent, therefore each of us deserves God's righteous punishment.

Explain that Jesus died to deal with our guilt and shame. He has taken our punishment on himself. Make it clear that those who have moved into a relationship with him are treated by God as if they are innocent.

Related Bible References

Romans 3:9–18 (no one is righteous); Psalm 44:20–21 (God knows the secrets of our hearts); Matthew 5:48 (call to be perfect as God is); Colossians 1:9–14 (moved into the kingdom of light), and Colossians 2:13–15 (law being set aside).

Other Ideas

Presumed Innocent also could set the stage for a talk on justice or a discussion that focuses on defining what sin actually entails (accepted taboos, conscious evil behavior, and/or attitudes of the heart).

Jared Reed

58
Pretty Woman

- R
- 119 minutes
- A 1990 film

Synopsis and Review

Pretty Woman set income records in theaters and video sales and launched Julia Roberts into superstar status. The movie uses the familiar rags to riches plot about two people from opposite economic, educational, and social positions teaching each other something important about life and eventually falling in love.

Edward Lewis (Richard Gere) is a wealthy corporate mogul who meets Vivian Ward (Julia Roberts) on Hollywood Boulevard where she is working as a prostitute. He buys her time for a week of companionship ($3000) and lavishes her with gifts and clothes.

The humor of the movie is built around Vivian the prostitute trying to adapt to the manners and ways of high society.

Vivian teaches Edward that love is a better investment than any corporate deal and shares her childhood dream about being rescued by a prince in shining armor. Edward reforms his business dealings and overcomes his fears to pursue love, eventually climbing the fire escape of Vivian's apartment building to "rescue" her and live happily ever after.

Suggestions for Viewing

There are two major "fantasy" scenes that most teenage fans of this movie love to watch.

1. The shopping spree scene (four minutes and ten seconds) is approximately halfway into the film. It immediately follows the scene where Edward is playing the piano in a deserted hotel ballroom, leading to a passionate scene with Vivian. The shopping spree begins with Edward saying, "Wake up. Time to shop!" Follow the scene until the "Pretty Woman" music finishes.

2. The prince rescuing the princess scene is the last ten minutes of the movie. It immediately follows the scene when Edward's lawyer, Stucky, attacks Vivian and is beaten up by Edward. Edward and Vivian talk about her leaving. She leaves. He finds her and fulfills her childhood dreams.

Important Scenes and/or Quotes

During the last ten minutes of the film, Edward and Vivian are trying to decide how to separate. They have completed their one-week contract. Edward is leaving for New York the next morning, and he asks Vivian what she wants. She says that she wants more.

> **Edward:** Wanting more? I invented the concept. How much more?
> **Vivian:** I want the fairy tale.

Vivian leaves the hotel and returns to her old apartment and roommate (also a prostitute) to discuss her future plans. Edward discovers her whereabouts and rides in his limo to her apartment. He scales the fire escape and "rescues" her with a kiss. Down on the street a Hollywood Boulevard "regular" is shouting his usual routine.

> Welcome to Hollywood! What's your dream? Everybody who comes to Hollywood has a dream. This is the land of dreams. Some come true; some don't. But keep on dreaming. This is Hollywood. There's always time to dream.

Music. End of movie.

Discussion Questions

What in this film made you feel good?

What in this movie is realistic and what is fantasy?

What's wrong with a movie that lets everything turn out happy and wonderful for everyone in the end?

Comment: The original script writer for this film appeared on ABC's 20/20 news program and complained that his script had been significantly changed during the filming of the movie. Two of the major differences were: 1) Vivian was a drug addict; and 2) Vivian threw the money in Edward's face (when they parted in the hotel) and returned to her life as a prostitute on the streets.

Garry Marshall, director of *Pretty Woman* acknowledged the changes and stated that the movie audiences did not want to see reality. They like happy endings, so that is what they were given.

What are some of the realities of life (prostitution, drug addiction, relationships, etc.) that were left out of this movie?

Why does the public want to watch fantasy, not reality?

What major changes do Vivian and Edward go through in one week (according to this movie)? Is it fantasy or reality? What makes real change happen in a person's life?

Outline of Talk or Wrap-up

Pretty Woman is a movie about major changes. Edward changes from a money-hungry corporate raider who is incapable of love to a compassionate compromiser who learns to stop and enjoy the simple pleasures of life. He also overcomes his fears of love (and his fear of heights) to rescue Vivian and give her a new life with him.

Vivian changes from a prostitute with no manners or class to an elegant lady. She stops believing all the bad stuff about herself and sets a new direction for her life. Amazing!

Is change that easy? Should we just keep dreaming and hope that someday it will come true? Does it matter that what we are doing (in Vivian's case, working as a prostitute) might be hurting both us and others as well as breaking God's laws for life?

Captivated by streetwise Vivian Ward (Julia Roberts, left), millionaire/corporate pirate Edward Lewis (Richard Gere, right) impulsively maneuvers a friendly takeover of Vivian's life.

After being coached in the ways of high society, the Cinderella of Hollywood Boulevard accompanies Edward as he moves through his world of extravagance and power.

You almost get the feeling that both Edward and Vivian have won the lottery. Instead of winning money, they have won love and happiness and new direction. They were doing the wrong thing (Vivian turning tricks and Edward buying her services and companionship), but they hit the jackpot and everything turned out great. So the message seems to be that if you do the wrong thing often enough, eventually you will get lucky and hit the big payoff.

The Bible is full of stories about people who went through some enormous changes in both attitude and action. The key to the change God can bring about in our lives starts with humility and repentance. First we acknowledge our need for God and his forgiveness. We turn from our sinful habits and lifestyles and try with God's help to please him with new attitudes and actions.

Don't be fooled, this change isn't quick or easy either. God has created the world and each of us to live under some clear principles: 1) Our life is a product of the investments we make. What we put in is what we get out. Galatians 6:7 says, "Do not be deceived. God cannot be mocked. A man reaps what he sows." 2) We can have a new start in life when we come to know Jesus Christ (Read 2 Cor. 5:17). God doesn't take away all of our problems or remove all the scars, but he does forgive us of every sin and begin renovating our attitudes and actions like a new owner fixing up a run-down house.

Don't just dream or fantasize about the changes you want to see in your life, let Jesus Christ do more than put you in fancy clothes. He can work a real change in you from the inside out.

Related Bible References

Ephesians 4:17–24; Colossians 3:1–17; 2 Corinthians 6:9–11; Luke 15:17 (lost son's attitude that brought change); Judges 16:1–30 (Samson's destruction because of his bad habits and restoration of his strength by change in his attitude); Luke 19 (Zacchaeus changes when he meets Jesus).

Jack Crabtree

59
The Princess Bride

- PG
- 98 minutes
- A 1987 film

Synopsis and Review

The Princess Bride uses a story-within-a-story approach where an uncle (Peter Falk) visits his sick nephew (Fred Savage) and reads him a book. The young boy is reluctant (there are a couple of interruptions during the reading of the story) but is gradually won over by the adventure. Rob Reiner, who directed this film, is known for his sense of comedy and this effort is a fine example. While some of the action borders on slapstick, for the most part the humor is built on funny lines and visual surprises. The characters are not at all complex, but they are very memorable, from the Spanish master swordsman, Inigo Montoya, to the dreaded pirate Roberts and the dangers of the fire-swamp. This is the hero-rescues-and-marries-the-princess story told with wonderful hilarity.

The underlying theme of *Princess* is the idea that "Nothing can stop true love." In the film, it turns out that not even death (or mostly death) can stop true love. It is improbable that Reiner was trying to make any theological points with his movie, but even a humorous look at love may open new views on the nature of human love and God's love.

Suggestions for Viewing

This is a great film for watching from beginning to end with the family or youth group. Although there are scary moments, the violence is minimal and not bloody. And there is only one obscenity uttered in the movie. When Inigo the Spanish swordsman finally meets his father's killer in a duel, he curses his enemy as he avenges his father's death. A three-second fast forward will pass by this section.

In a youth group, you may want to introduce this film by separating the males and females and having each group come up with a list of "What has to happen in a really great love story." Then bring them back together to share their lists with each other. The differences will probably spark a great discussion. Move into the film by encouraging them to compare the love story they are about to see with the lists they just compiled.

Offer a reward for the person who can come up with the best line from the film.

Important Scenes and/or Quotes

1. This film could probably be analyzed as a cleverly strung together series of skits. The most memorable ones are the three challenges that the hero Westley must overcome: the skill of the swordsman, the strength of the giant, and the pompous intelligence of the arch-criminal.
2. Westley and Princess Buttercup's adventure in the fire-swamp involves an interesting kind of grim humor.
3. Later, Westley experiences "ultimate suffering" at the hands of Prince Humperdink. Thinking he is dead, his friends take him to "Miracle Max," played superbly by Billy Crystal.
4. The fake marriage scene is also worth a chuckle or two. As is true of all love stories, the hero rescues the princess, and they live happily ever after.

Discussion Questions

What did you think was the funniest scene in this film? (When you preview it, reset your VCR counter so you can note the numbers at the memorable scenes. If there is a consensus on several sections the group wants to review, you will be able to rewind to that point.)

If you could act, which part would you have enjoyed playing in this story?

How many of the points you came up with earlier about a great love story were part of this film?

If you had to come up with a definition of "true love" from this movie, what ideas would you use?

Outline of Talk or Wrap-up

Clues that true love is present:

a desire to say "As you wish" to someone else

a willingness to wait for the right time

a willingness to be faithful

pursuing/courting the one who is loved

valuing and honoring (i.e. respecting) the one who is loved

marriage is only the beginning of the real story

Related Bible References

If you wish to use this movie as an unusual way to introduce the gospel, here is a possible text: Colossians 1:9–14 (being rescued from Satan's kingdom). For a discussion of "true love," use 1 Corinthians 13.

Neil Wilson

60
Rain Man

- R
- 140 minutes
- A 1988 film

Synopsis and Review

Rain Man won a number of Oscars, including Best Picture and Best Actor (Dustin Hoffman). The story centers on a self-centered, money-hungry, manipulative young man, Charlie Babbitt (Tom Cruise), who returns to Cincinnati from Los Angeles to attend his father's funeral. To his surprise, his wealthy father, from whom he has been estranged, leaves him only a car and gives the remaining $3 million to a foundation for the mentally ill. Preparing to challenge the institution for his right to the money, Charlie discovers his autistic brother, Raymond (Dustin Hoffman), whom he never knew, living in the institution.

As a ploy to recover his share of the inheritance, Charlie kidnaps his brother and begins a cross-country road trip back to L.A. Along the way, he makes demands and negotiates a financial settlement with the director of the institution, Dr. Bruner (Jerry Molen).

When Charlie discovers Raymond's uncanny ability to remember numbers, he teaches him to play blackjack. In Las Vegas, using Raymond's ability, Charlie wins enough money to repay his pressing business debts.

The car trip and the stop in Las Vegas give the impatient, unloving Charlie a new sensitivity and appreciation for his autistic brother. On reaching L.A., Charlie realizes his inability to care for his brother and turns him over to authorities to return him to the institution in Cincinnati.

Suggestions for Viewing

1. First night at the hotel/Charlie's girlfriend, Susanna (Valeria Golino), walks out (eight minutes). This is a powerful scene. It is somewhat graphic and filled with bad language, but it shows Charlie being rebuked by his girlfriend for using Raymond and lying constantly to get what he wants.

   Charlie takes Raymond from the institution (driving over the bridge) and checks into a hotel. Raymond walks in on Charlie and his girlfriend having sex. The next scene Charlie goes into Raymond's room to yell at him. Start the video here.

   An argument ensues between Charlie and his girlfriend (plenty of bad language). She exposes Charlie as a lying, self-centered man who would say or do anything to protect his best interest. She packs her bags and walks out. Raymond remains sitting on the bed oblivious to the whole scene. Stop the video here.

2. The trip to Las Vegas (eleven min.) Approximately one hundred minutes into the movie, Charlie and Raymond are in a laundromat. Charlie gets the bad news that he has to pay back the $80,000 someone gave him as a down payment on a Lamborghini. They drive through Las Vegas and check into a motel.

   Start the video at the beginning of the next scene when they are eating breakfast in a diner. Raymond is playing with a jukebox selector at the table. Charlie recognizes Raymond's unusual ability to memorize and devises a scheme to use Raymond to win money at the blackjack tables in Las Vegas.

   Continue through their entry into Las Vegas and their play at the blackjack table. After they lose $3,000 on the roulette wheel, they relax at the bar. Charlie is counting the money "they" won that will pay his business debts. As he gets ready to leave Raymond at the bar he says, "While I'm gone the sign says don't walk." Stop the video at that point.

Warning: this film is rated R because of the language, a simulated sex scene, and adult themes.

Important Scenes and/or Quotes

See above.

Discussion Questions

What was Charlie's primary motive when he kidnapped his brother and when he taught him how to play blackjack?

Imagine that you were a third sibling with Charlie and Raymond. What would you think about your brother kidnapping your other brother? How would the amount of inheritance you received affect your attitude?

In what way was Charlie using his brother for his own interests? What concerns did he have for what was best for his brother?

Describe any situations where you have seen someone use a friend or family member for their own interests. When have you felt used by someone else?

What would cause a person to change from using someone to really loving him or her? How would the person's actions and attitudes have to change?

Outline for Talk or Wrap-up

The greatest compliment you can give to friends is to say that they are always there when you need them. The worst put-down you can give them is to say that they are always there when they need you.

That statement points out the vital ingredient in a good relationship (with family or friends). Are we in the relationship to give or to take?

It has been said that one of the greatest perversions of life is when we love things and use people rather than love people and use things. Charlie Babbitt was certainly a good example of using people in the scenes we watched from this movie.

We are quick to notice when other people use us, but we often don't recognize when we use others for our own selfish purposes. We justify whatever we do as necessary for our success and minimize whatever hurt we inflict on others.

Jesus said we are to love our neighbors as we love ourselves.

That simple and clear standard will help us decide if we are guilty of using others or really loving them.

Love is a well-worn word in our culture. Sometimes telling someone we love them means very little. How many times have we seen someone take advantage of a boyfriend or girlfriend in the name of love? Have you ever seen someone declare love and loyalty to a friend and then disappear when the going gets tough?

Try defining love this way: "I love you!" means being willing to do whatever is best for the other person no matter what it costs you. In your relationships, can you honestly say you think about what is the absolute best for the other person and give them the treatment you would want for yourself?

Jesus Christ not only talked about love, he provided the ultimate example. He knew our greatest need was forgiveness from God for our sins. Although he knew it would cost him his life, he willingly laid down his life so that we could be forgiven and made right in the sight of God. In addition to that ultimate sacrifice, he also demonstrated that kind of love when he washed the disciples' feet and gave his full attention to everyone who needed his help.

None of us can match Jesus' perfect example, but we can let his genuine love come into and flow from our lives. Jesus challenged his disciples again and again to stop thinking about themselves and begin thinking about how they could meet the needs of others.

If Jesus were to challenge you, which of your relationships would he want to change? Don't be afraid to really love people. It sure beats using them.

Related Bible References

Matthew 19:19; Mark 12:28–34; John 15:1–17; John 13:1–17; Luke 10:25–37 (Good Samaritan); Romans 12:3–21; Philippians 2:3–5.

Jack Crabtree

61
Rocky III

- PG
- 99 minutes
- A 1982 film

Synopsis and Review

This third installment in the *Rocky* series focuses on fear and believing in yourself. After beating Apollo Creed (Carl Weathers), Rocky (Sylvester Stallone) has enjoyed a few years of fame and fortune. When he is challenged to a title fight by the hard-hitting Clubber Lang (Mr. T), he is suddenly faced with a new emotion—fear. He must find out who he is and how to confront his fears.

The film follows the typical Rocky pattern: fighter is challenged, fighter struggles to overcome obstacles, fighter wins. Yet, it is hard not to be moved by watching the underdog triumph again. With the beautiful photography and stirring musical score, you find yourself cheering Rocky on to another victory.

Suggestions for Viewing

Because of its popularity, most people may have already seen *Rocky III*. It is worth seeing again because it points out the worthlessness of wealth and fame. It is possible to show specific scenes for discussion.

Warning: *Rocky III* contains some offensive language and violent boxing scenes.

Important Scenes and/or Quotes

Near the beginning of the film, Rocky has enlisted Apollo Creed's help in training to fight Clubber Lang.

Having previously fought and lost to Lang, Rocky struggles through the training. He is also dealing with the death of his former trainer and the allegations that his previous title matches were carried bouts. He has just decided to quit when his wife, Adrienne (Talia Shire) confronts him about his reasons for quitting.

Adrienne: It was real.

Rocky: Nothing is real if you don't believe in who you are. I don't believe in myself no more. Don't you understand? When a fighter don't believe in himself, it's over. He's finished. That's it.

Adrienne: That's not it.

Rocky: That is it.

Adrienne: Why don't you tell me the truth?

Rocky: What are you putting me through here, Adrienne? You wanna know the truth. The truth is I don't wanna lose what I got. I used to not care about what happened to me. I'd go in the ring, get busted up, I didn't care. But now there's you, the kid. I don't want to lose what I got.

Adrienne: What do we got that can't be replaced? What? A house? We got cars; we got money. We got everything but the truth. What's the truth?

Rocky: I'm afraid. You wanna hear me say it? You wanna break me down. All right. I'm afraid. For the first time in my life, I'm afraid.

Adrienne: I'm afraid, too. There is nothing wrong with being afraid.

Rocky: There is. For me there is.

Adrienne: Why? You're human, aren't you?

Rocky: I don't know what I am. All I know is that I'm a liar. And because of that, Mickey ain't here no more.

Adrienne: You didn't push him into anything. He was a grown man. He did what he had to do. And you have no right to feel guilty for what happened. You don't. You're gonna tell me those fights weren't real. That you were carried. Well, I don't believe it. But it doesn't matter what I believe because you're the one that's gotta carry the fear around inside you. Afraid that everybody's gonna take things away. Afraid that everybody's gonna think that you are a coward, that you're not a man anymore. None of it's true. But it doesn't matter if I tell you because you're the one that's gotta settle it. Get rid of it. Because when all the smoke is cleared, when all the people quit chanting your name, it's just gonna be us. And you can't live like this. We can't live like this. Apollo thinks you can do it. So do I, but you gotta want to do it for the right reasons. Not for the guilt over Mickey, not the money, not for the title, not for me, but for you. Just you.

Rocky: And if I lose . . .?

Adrienne: Then you lose. At least you lose with no excuses, no fear. You can live with that.

Discussion Questions

What are some of the fears that keep people from taking risks?

Why is it so hard to admit that we are afraid?

What things are we afraid of losing?

Adrienne tells Rocky that he has to fight for the right reasons. What are the right reasons? The wrong reasons?

What kinds of risks do we take as Christians?

What kinds of fears might we encounter?

How does God deal with our fears?

How could God deal with your specific fears?

Outline of Talk or Wrap-up

This scene from *Rocky* illustrates that even the strongest men can feel fear so strongly that they would want to quit. Use biblical illustrations to show how God uses the unlikeliest of people to accomplish great things. Stress the point that God not only makes it physically possible, he also makes it mentally possible. God gives us the confidence in ourselves to accomplish the impossible. When we learn that as children of God, we are the best that can be, we learn to believe in ourselves. Then and only then can we be true fighters for the Lord.

Talk about the healthy nature of fear. Even Jesus was afraid of the cross. Fear causes us to ask intelligent questions, examine our motives, and determine the value of the goal. If we follow Jesus' example, we go to the Lord in prayer and place our fears in his hands. Then we get up off our knees and go slay a few giants!

Related Bible References

Psalm 27:1–2; Luke 22:39–46; John 16:33; Matthew 10:26, 31.

Tim and Patty Atkins

62

Roxanne

- PG
- 107 minutes
- A 1987 film based on the play *Cyrano de Bergerac* by Edmond Rostand

Synopsis and Review

As in *Cyrano de Bergerac*, the main character in *Roxanne*, Charlie "C.D." Bales (Steve Martin) has an exceptionally large nose. C.D., who is tremendously talented and well-liked, lives in a small ski resort town in the northwest where he serves as fire chief. His only liability seems to be his huge nose. When beautiful Roxanne (Daryl Hannah) moves into town for the summer, C.D. is entranced. But he knows that Roxanne would never be interested in him because of his nose. At the same time, there is a new, young fireman, Chris McDonnell (Rick Rossovich), who is quite handsome, but very shy and inarticulate—Roxanne seems to have her eyes on him. C.D. helps this young man express his feelings for Roxanne by writing love notes to her from him. In these notes, however, C.D. is really expressing his own feelings. Overwhelmed by the romantic notes, Roxanne falls for the fireman, thinking that he must be the sensitive author. Eventually the deception is exposed as are C.D.'s feelings for Roxanne.

Suggestions for Viewing

The best use of *Roxanne* is to show key scenes and to discuss them. It is rated PG primarily due to the references to sex, so be sure to preview the film. C.D.'s attitudes toward his nose can be quite instructive of our own deficiencies, real or perceived. There is a lot of humor, and Steve Martin is in prime form.

Important Scenes and Discussion Questions

1. Set the stage, explaining C.D.'s unusual nose and his position in town. Show the scene, near the beginning of the movie, where two men encounter C.D. on the sidewalk and make fun of his nose. At the conclusion of this sidewalk showdown, pause the video.

    How do we know that C.D. is sensitive about his nose?

    What other things were the two guys making fun of?

    In what ways did C.D. try to avoid a confrontation?

2. Fast forward to the scene where C.D. has just let Roxanne into the house after she accidentally locked herself out. Begin where they start talking. Roxanne has a great line in the dialogue. She says, "Would you like some wine with your nose?" C.D. begins to fall in love with her. Stop when he closes the door.

    Before showing this scene, divide the group in half. Explain that this is the first time Roxanne has seen C.D. Ask one group to watch Roxanne's reaction to the situation. Have the other group pay close attention to how C.D. handles meeting someone new.

    How well do you think Roxanne handled the situation?

    How did C.D. react to someone new?

    How conscious was C.D. of his nose?

3. Next, move to the firehouse when the men are warning the new recruit, Chris McDonnell, not to say anything about C.D.'s nose. They are trying to prepare Chris for the enormity of C.D.'s nose. The scene takes place around the firehouse pool table.

    Why did the firemen warn Chris about C.D.'s nose?

    When have you been warned about someone's idiosyncrasy?

4. Move to the restaurant scene where C.D.'s friend is telling him to ask Roxanne out. C.D. hears that Roxanne is in love with someone. C.D. thinks that Roxanne is in love with him, but in reality, she is interested in Chris. Also show the scene where Chris sees C.D.'s nose for the first time.

Why didn't C.D. get angry with the new recruit? (Because he thought Roxanne was accepting him.)

How would C.D. usually have reacted?

How can our acceptance of others affect their outlook on life?

5. A very funny fireman-training scene follows. Then Roxanne and C.D. hike up a mountain, and C.D. finds out that he is not the object of her love. He is crushed and begins to dream about having a different nose. He talks to his doctor about a nose job. Show the training scene, the hiking scene, and the doctor's office scene.

When C.D.'s friend encouraged him to ask Roxanne out, how did he react?

How would life for C.D. change if he were to get the nose job? How might his personality change? (C.D. is talented, funny, athletic, warm, and a community leader, etc. Maybe he wouldn't have developed this way with a "cute little button nose.")

6. The movie ends after Roxanne really does come to love and accept C.D., nose and all. They live happily ever after.

Outline of Talk or Wrap-up

1. No one is perfect. Everyone has physical or character traits they would like to change.

2. Many people have overcome great shortcomings to accomplish great achievements: Abe Lincoln is thought to have suffered from Marfan's Syndrome (a cardiac disease making him 6'4" at age 14); Thomas Edison's mom yanked him out of school in the first grade because he didn't seem capable of doing the work; Mario Andretti, one of the world's most successful racecar drivers of all time, is less than 5 1/2 feet tall; Jim Abbott, a premiere major league pitcher, uses one arm—he's missing the hand on his other arm.

3. Accepting your own self-worth is easier when someone accepts you as Roxanne did C.D. Jesus Christ accepts you totally as his very own child (see John 1:12).

4. Illustration: hold up a loaf of bread. Ask group members

how much they would pay for it (about 79 cents). Ask if they would pay any more. Any less? How about this boom box? (Ask same questions). Explain that they probably will only pay what the object is worth to the purchaser. No more and no less. Then ask: "What are you worth? Someone thought you were worth the ultimate price—death on the cross" (see 1 Cor. 6:19–20).

Related Bible References

1 Samuel 16:7; Luke 16:15; Romans 8:31, 38–39; 1 John 4:11, 19.

Gary Schulte

63
Sophie's Choice

- R
- 155 minutes
- A 1982 film based on the novel by William Styron

Synopsis and Review

Sophie's Choice is about Sophie Zawistowska (Meryl Streep), a Polish immigrant who survived the Holocaust. Set in post-war Brooklyn in 1947, *Sophie* chronicles the adventure of the discovery of an aspiring novelist, the film's narrator, Stingo (Peter MacNicol). Twenty-two-year-old Stingo, a self-admitted stranger to love and death, has moved to New York from rural Virginia to discover life and to write a novel. He ends up renting a room in the same house where Sophie and her eccentric lover Nathan (Kevin Kline) happen to share the room above his.

Stingo is young, naive, and inexperienced. Sophie, who is worldly-wise, is struggling to cope with a past that is riddled with disappointments resulting from decisions that have shaped her life. Nathan, who rescued Sophie shortly after she arrived in New York, is a mystery who is slowly revealed to be a paranoid schizophrenic, addicted to cocaine.

Sophie's life is unraveled through a series of dialogues with Stingo. In war-torn Poland, she is shaken out of complacency by the discovery that her father is a Jew hater. Captured by the Nazis, she is forced to choose between either saving the life of her daughter or her son. In Auschwitz she must decide whether she will attempt to save her son or aid the Resistance.

As the movie progresses, Stingo falls in love with Sophie who is at least ten years his senior. Realizing Nathan's destructive and volatile nature, Stingo tries to persuade Sophie to escape with him to a farm in Virginia. In the end, Sophie's past and Nathan's psychological condition become too much of a burden for either one of them to bear, so they kill themselves in a double suicide. This leaves Stingo to reflect on his strange acquaintance with both love and death through his encounter with Sophie.

Suggestions for Viewing

Sophie is a long movie containing strong language that may be objectionable. *Sophie* also contains some sexually suggestive scenes, though none of them involve nudity. Two such scenes stand out: (1) Stingo's date, early in the film; (2) Stingo and Sophie's hotel scene at the end of the movie. Previewing this film is recommended. Seen in its entirety *Sophie* is a powerful film; however, a plot summary used with a few dramatic scenes (outlined below) is probably more appropriate.

Important Scenes and/or Quotes

Sophie is packed with powerful displays of human emotion. The most potent scenes are Sophie's flashbacks of the events and decisions that have shaped her life. The two most profound are:

1. The scene about halfway through the film when Stingo confronts Sophie about her account of her father's anti-semitic activity. She describes her profound disappointment when she is awakened from her life of comfort with the revelation that her father advocates the extermination of Jews in Poland. This scene flows into her account of how her husband left her, how she became involved with a member of the Jewish Resistance, and her eventual arrest by the Nazis. This is followed by another dramatic scene of decisions in Auschwitz where Sophie is consumed with the thought of saving her son who has also been imprisoned. Both her attempt to steal a radio for the Resistance and her willingness to become involved with Rudolf Hess to save her son are revealing.

2. The scene in which Sophie has gone away with Stingo to escape Nathan who has threatened to kill them both because he suspects them of infidelity. Stingo has asked Sophie to marry him and bear his children. Sophie responds with an account of how she was forced to decide whom she would save from death, her son or her daughter. This decision haunts and consumes her.

Discussion Questions

What choices did Sophie really have? How would you have dealt with the choices with which Sophie was confronted?

How does Sophie try to rebuild her post-war life in New York? What is wrong with her strategy?

In what ways do we deny our past and our feelings to get on with life?

Why was it so hard for Sophie to face the truth about her past?

Why is self-deception a poor strategy for dealing with life?

How does the forgiveness offered to us in Christ's death answer our need to deal with our past mistakes?

What does this movie have to say about the fairness of life? Is life fair?

Outline of Talk or Wrap-up

Use *Sophie* to explore the following themes:

1. All choices and decisions have consequences. Bad choices tend to haunt us. We need to choose carefully between wisdom and folly.
2. Suppressed guilt (true or false) consumes. Sophie was ultimately destroyed by feelings of immense guilt about her choices. Only the forgiveness found in Christ can adequately handle our guilt.
3. People (even believers) attempt to make life work according to their own foolishness. Sophie finds comfort and security in lies and self-denial. She is afraid that if anyone knew about her and the choice that she had been forced to make, they wouldn't accept (love) her. Real

comfort and security are found in a relationship with God that is possible only when we face the truth about ourselves.

4. Life is difficult and often unfair. As believers, our hope has to be in God, believing that he will, in the end, right all wrongs.

Related Bible References

Jeremiah 2:13 (how people attempt to make life work according to their own agenda apart from God); Jeremiah 17:9 (the heart is deceitful); Ephesians 1:7; Colossians 1:14 (forgiveness and redemption are available in Christ); Proverbs 8:32–36 (wisdom and foolishness, death); John 8:32 (the importance of truth that leads to freedom).

Robert Eugene DiPaolo

64

Stand By Me

- R
- 87 minutes
- A 1986 film

Synopsis and Review

This Rob Reiner film is one of the best looks at pre-adolescent relationships ever made. A cast of four young stars, Wil Wheaton as Gordie Lachance, River Phoenix as Chris Chambers, Corey Feldman as Teddy Duchamp, and Jerry O'Connell as Vein Tessio, portray the full gamut of pre-teen emotions—joy, fear, anger, sorrow, and compassion.

The story line is simple, and rather secondary to the relational interaction that gives the film value. A boy from their 1950s town has been missing for days. A rumor spreads that his dead body was spotted in a remote location. The boys push each other into agreeing that they want to see the body, and they subsequently set out along railroad tracks that will lead them to the spot. On the way they learn much about each other, about friendship, and about growing up.

Suggestions for Viewing

Warning: To be fully honest, *Stand By Me* is filled with swearing and vulgar language. There's probably not a youth pastor in the nation who could show it to his youth group without taking the risk of an emergency church board meeting the following evening. Parents, however, could watch the entire film with their children.

Stand By Me is truly enjoyable. One scene in particular

can be used on its own. It is presented below, and the discussion questions that follow are tied to this scene.

Important Scenes and/or Quotes

One usable scene deals with how other peoples' expectations of us play a major role in who we are and who we become. The scene can be found about forty minutes into the film. The boys are trying to sleep around a campfire. Because they are nervous, they've decided to stand watch in shifts. While Chris Chambers (the leader of the group, played by River Phoenix) is on duty, Gordie Lachance (Wil Wheaton) wakes up and the two have a talk about Chris's future.

> **Gordie:** You could go into the college courses with me (referring to their upcoming seventh grade year).
> **Chris:** That'll be the day.
> **Gordie:** Why not? You're smart enough.
> **Chris:** They won't let me.
> **Gordie:** Whadya mean?
> **Chris:** That's the way people think of my family in this town—it's the way they think of me. I'm just one of those low-life Chambers kids.
> **Gordie:** That's not true.
> **Chris:** Oh, it is. . . .

The conversation goes on for another minute or two while Chris builds a case for the fact that he doesn't seem to have a chance in life—merely because of everyone's expectations. Watching the scene a few times by yourself before you show it will enable you to know exactly where to stop the tape to avoid language you'd rather not let your students hear. Or, warn your kids of the language, and explain the context.

Chris's final words in the scene are powerful. Through tears he sobs: "I wish I could just go someplace where nobody knows me!"

Discussion Questions

The following questions relate to the scene described above.

What, specifically, were the expectations being placed on Chris? And why do you suppose those expectations were there?

When have you felt like Chris, that you had to act a certain way because people expected you to? What was it about their expectations that made them seem so demanding?

List five people whose opinions matter to you.

In what ways are students in your school swayed to act certain ways by fellow classmates' expectations?

Outline of Talk or Wrap-up

After showing the clip and working through the discussion questions, talk to students about God's approval. Stress that God made them perfect in his eyes. And while it's important to try to be our best for God, we don't need to go through life trying to seek his approval—we already have it.

Explain that it's very important to decide whom we'll listen to and whom we won't. Everyone has an opinion, and many are willing to share theirs with us. We can go through life on the whims of other people's comments and expectations if we don't decide beforehand whom we'll listen to. Obviously, we should listen to God first.

Related Bible References

On peer pressure and expectations: Exodus 23:2; Mark 12:31; John 15:18–21; Ephesians 1:11–12; Luke 17:1; 2 Samuel 16:16–23; James 4:4. On friendship: 2 Samuel 1:23; John 15:12–17; Ecclesiastes 4:9–12; 2 Timothy 1:16–18.

Other Ideas

If you watch the whole movie, there are scores of other topics you can discuss. On a surface level, you can ask students if these boys accurately portrayed what goes on in the minds and discussions of today's young teens. In addition, you can talk about friendships—how they last and how they don't; what makes good friendships; being vulnerable with friends. You can also discuss using the gifts God has given us.

Mark Oestreicher

65
Star Trek V: The Final Frontier

- PG
- 106 minutes
- A 1989 film

Synopsis and Review

This installment of the Star Trek movies reunites all the familiar characters in a new adventure. The Enterprise is hijacked by a Vulcan named Sybok (Laurence Luckinbill), Spock's half-brother, who is determined to use it on a journey to discover the universe's innermost spiritual secrets.

The movie maintains all the usual Star Trek traditions of special effects and science fiction adventure. It also contains a fair amount of humor. The most intriguing part of the movie is that it explores a variety of views on spirituality.

Suggestions for Viewing

Star Trek V is enjoyable to watch in its entirety for entertainment alone. For the sake of discussion, however, the pivotal scene occurs when Captain Kirk (William Shatner), Bones (DeForest Kelly), Spock (Leonard Nimoy), and the Vulcan encounter a being they believe to be God.

Star Trek V contains a small amount of offensive language.

Important Scenes and/or Quotes

Having successfully piloted to the center of the galaxy, Captain Kirk, Bones, Spock, and the Vulcan meet a being who identifies himself as God.

God: Brave souls. Welcome.

Bones: Is this the voice of God?

God: One voice, many faces. (Creates an old man face) Does this better suit your expectations?

Vulcan: God.

God: It is I. The journey you took to reach me could not have been an easy one.

Vulcan: It was not. The Barrier stood between us, but we breached it.

God: Magnificent! You are the first to reach me.

Vulcan: We only sought your infinite wisdom.

God: And how did you breach this Barrier?

Vulcan: With a starship.

God: This starship, could it carry my wisdom beyond the Barrier?

Vulcan: It could, yes.

God: Then I will make use of this starship.

Vulcan: It will be your chariot.

Kirk: Excuse me.

God: It will carry my power to every corner of creation.

Kirk: Excuse me. I'd just like to ask a question. What does God need with a starship?

God: Bring the ship closer.

Kirk: I said, What does God need with a starship?

Bones: Jim, what are you doing?

Kirk: I'm asking a question.

God: Who is this creature?

Kirk: Who am I? Don't you know? Aren't you God?

Vulcan: He has his doubts.

God: You doubt me?

Kirk: I seek proof.

Bones: Jim, you don't ask the Almighty for his I.D.

God: Then here's the proof that you seek. (He zaps Kirk off his feet.)

Kirk: Why is God angry?

Vulcan: What have you done to my friend?

God: He doubts me.

The original *Star Trek* characters are reunited. They are (from left) Mr. Spock (Leonard Nimoy), Sulu (George Takei), Chekov (Walter Koenig), Captain James T. Kirk (William Shatner, seated), "Scotty" (James Doohan), Dr. Leonard "Bones" McCoy (DeForest Kelley), and Uhura (Nichelle Nichols).

Spock: You've not answered his question. What does God need with a starship? (God zaps Spock)

God: Do you doubt me?

Bones: I doubt any God who inflicts pain for his pleasure.

The scene continues and it is revealed that the being is really an evil force who has been imprisoned in that place.

Discussion Questions

Ask these questions following the scene described above.

Were the characters questioning or doubting? What's the difference?

Do we have the right to question God?

Do you know people who are so blind in their faith that they would believe anything about a god or doctrine?

Why are we so easily fooled or convinced in our faith?

What does the Bible tell us about God's relationship to pain?

How have questioners changed history? The Church?

Why are Christians so intolerant of doubters?

Why does society seem more tolerant?

In the movie, the image of God fell apart in the face of questions. How does the real God do in the face of questions? How does your faith stand up to questioning?

Outline of Talk or Wrap-up

This scene is a great illustration of the believability and sincerity of God. Point out the importance of questions and the dangers of blind faith. Use biblical illustrations to show how God answered believers' questions. Emphasize the point that God does not want blind obedience. Rather, he wants deep conviction and understanding.

Talk about the proof God offers us. God doesn't have to resort to violence in the face of questions because he has the answers. And these answers can be found in the Bible. The Bible is a handbook of proof. Discuss other proofs such as the miracle of creation.

Related Bible References

Matthew 17:20; Luke 24:38; Job 6:10; Matthew 21:21; Luke 22:32; Ecclesiastes 1:17–18; Matthew 14:31; James 1:3.

Other Ideas

This same scene can be used to discuss the idea of pain and its origin. It can also be used to discuss God's anger and how it affects us.

Tim and Patty Atkins

66
Tender Mercies

- PG
- 93 minutes
- A 1983 film

Synopsis and Review

Tender Mercies is a realistic movie about an alcoholic's road to recovery. Mac Sledge (Robert Duvall) is a country singer at the end of his road. Once a big star, he is now on the verge of drinking himself to death. Mac ends up at a motel where he offers to work for his room and board. The motel is owned by a young widow named Rosa Lee (Tess Harper) who agrees to Sledge's offer but makes it a requirement that he no longer drink. He agrees.

Unlike many attempts at throwing off addictions, Sledge's recovery is pretty much a straight road back. He falls for the widow who runs the motel, and they marry. Eventually he and her son are baptized, a result of her strength of character and religious conviction. This is a far cry from his high-profile, high-glamor country music career, but then that's the way he likes it.

Sledge still has to cope with his past though. The local newspaper prints a story about him, and his country music friends keep dropping by. Later, Sledge's ex-wife enters the picture. And there are still unanswered questions in his mind about why his daughter died. Through Rosa, however, Sledge weathers these challenges.

Tender Mercies portrays conversion the way it really happens. It is an inspiring picture of how recovery and redemption can and does take place in our fallen world.

259

Suggestions for Viewing

Tender Mercies could be shown in its entirety, with a focus on drinking and its potential for destruction. Or you could show the scene described below and discuss God's mercy.

Warning: there is some strong language and violence.

Important Scenes and/or Quotes

As mentioned above, you could watch the entire film and discuss alcoholism.

One of the central themes of the movie is the tender mercy of God. The scene in which Sledge and Rosa are discussing the fairness of God would be an appropriate discussion starter. Include an appropriate introduction so that the students understand the context of the discussion.

The scene occurs when Sledge and Rosa are working in the field. Sledge asks why he, a man bent on self-destruction, was spared, while his daughter, who was seemingly innocent, ended up dying in a car accident. Rosa answers, "the tender mercies of God. . . ."

Discussion Questions

For a Discussion on Drinking

What are the dangers of drinking?

What makes a person an alcoholic?

How do you think Sledge became an alcoholic?

If you have an alcoholic in your family, what are some of the ways you can help him or her?

What can we learn about life and faith from Rosa?

For a Discussion on God's Mercy

In what ways did God display tender mercies to Sledge and his daughter?

What does the title, "Tender Mercies," mean?

How has God shown his mercy toward us?

How should we respond to God's mercy?

Outline of Talk or Wrap-up

For a discussion on drinking, invite a recovering alcoholic to come and tell what has enabled him or her to recover. Or, talk about why kids drink and the dangers of alcoholism.

For a discussion on God's mercy, say something like: "It can be hard to understand how some people who deserve punishment often escape while others become innocent victims. Instead of trying to explain why every apparent injustice occurs, we can find comfort in four truths.

"First of all, we don't know exactly why God allows certain events, and we never will. It's up to us to trust him. In fact, that's what faith is all about.

"Second, a lot of the bad things that happen to people are the result of a fallen world. Sin is a fact of life, as are the consequences of sin. And don't forget, because we're sinful, we often make very bad choices. Those have consequences too.

"Third, we should be thankful that God is merciful at all. No one is innocent—all of us deserve God's death penalty (Rom. 3:23; 6:23).

"Fourth, God holds back punishment so that the guilty can have time to repent (2 Peter 3:9). What great mercy God shows us!"

Related Bible References

Luke 1:77–80; Romans 5:6–8.

Bob Arnold

67
Terms of Endearment

- PG
- 132 minutes
- A 1983 film based on the novel by Larry McMurtry (won Academy Award for Best Picture)

Synopsis and Review

Terms of Endearment is a movie about relationships. It's primarily about the thirty-year love-hate relationship between a mother, Aurora Greenway (Shirley MacLaine) and her only daughter Emma (Debra Winger). The movie is also about other relationships. Aurora, whose husband died when Emma was a child develops a relationship with a retired astronaut, while being pursued by Vernon Dahlart (Danny DeVito).

The film follows carefree Emma's marriage to irresponsible Flapp Horton (Jeff Daniels) and their subsequent moves from Texas to Iowa to Nebraska. During this period Emma and Flapp have three children, much to the chagrin of Aurora, who believes in having all her ducks in a row. Flapp, who teaches college English, is pursing a graduate degree as well as other women. Emma experiences solace as well as guilt as she develops a relationship with an Iowa banker named Sam Burns (John Lithgow).

During this same period, the otherwise tightly wound Aurora begins to unwind as she develops a relationship with her eccentric next door neighbor, Garrett Breedlove (Jack Nicholson). Garrett is an ex-astronaut turned continual womanizer.

Shortly after moving to Nebraska, Emma discovers that she has cancer. This revelation brings together several loose ends as Emma and Aurora, Emma and Flapp, and Emma and her eldest son Tommy make amends. In the end, Emma dies and Flapp, conceding to his shortcomings and Emma's last wishes, allows Aurora to raise the children.

Suggestions for Viewing

Ideally, *Terms* should be watched in its entirety. It is a movie that progresses through the thirty-year relationship between Aurora and Emma. Though *Terms* is rated PG, it deals frankly with the subject of sex, contains some offensive language, and has a few suggestive scenes. Preview it before using it.

Important Scenes and/or Quotes

1. At the film's beginning, Emma says to her friend Patsy, "Sure would be nice to have a mother somebody liked."
2. The day before Emma marries Flapp, Aurora says, "You wouldn't want me to be silent about something even if it was for your own good. You are not special enough to overcome a bad marriage. Don't marry Flapp Horton."
3. Midway through the film, Emma calls Aurora to tell her she's pregnant for the third time and needs money. Aurora tells her to get an abortion. She says, "How is your life going to get better when you keep having babies with that man?"
4. Also about midway through the film, Flapp and Emma are having a fight. Tommy and Teddy take off. When Emma finds them, they explain that they didn't want people to think they lived there. Tommy tells her, "You're driving Daddy away."
5. Emma and Sam's contemplation and consummation of an affair.
6. Aurora tells Garret that she thinks it's sad that he has to use all his astronaut memorabilia to get women into the sack. Garret replies, "You need to use all your assets. Everybody uses everything they have. Sometimes it's not enough."
7. The contrast between Emma and Patsy in New York toward the end of the movie.

8. The scene of reconciliation and forgiveness between Emma and Flapp; Emma and Aurora; and Emma and Tommy.

Discussion Questions

With which character do you most identify: organized Aurora, carefree Emma, self-centered Flapp, go-for-the-gusto Garret, sensitive Sam Burns, or perfect (on the outside) Patsy? Explain your answer.

Compare and contrast two or more of the above characters. What motivates each one? How do they deal with crises? What would be their mottoes in life? (example—Garret: "You only go around once, so make the most of it," or, "You gotta use what ya got.")

What impact does Aurora have on Emma? How does Emma relate to her son Tommy? How does this affect him? How does Flapp's philandering affect Emma and their children? How does Garret change Aurora?

How does Emma's impending death affect or change her relationship with Aurora? Flapp? Tommy? How would you respond to the death of a close friend or family member?

Outline of Talk or Wrap-up

Terms is a difficult movie to categorize. Ultimately it is about relationships, delving into the world of fragile human relationships motivated by love, insecurity, hidden agenda, and fear. It also deals with how these relationships affect and damage people. Use the above scenes and quotes with the Scripture references below to generate discussion about the complexities of human relationships between friends (Emma and Patsy), men and women (Emma and Flapp, Aurora and Garret, Emma and Sam), and parents and children (Aurora and Emma, Emma and Tommy).

Related Bible References

Ecclesiastes 7:2–4 (the sobriety of death); Colossians 3:18–21 (family roles and relationships); 1 Samuel 18—20 (the healthy relationship between David and Jonathan); 1 John 4:18; 1 Peter

4:8 (the importance of love that drives out fear and covers sins); Jeremiah 2:13 (how people attempt to make life work according to their own agenda apart from God); and Ephesians 1:7; Colossians 1:14 (forgiveness and redemption are available in Christ).

Robert Eugene DiPaolo

68
To Kill a Mockingbird

- Unrated
- 129 minutes
- A 1962 film based on the best-selling novel by Harper Lee

Synopsis and Review

Macomb County, Alabama is the setting for this drama about prejudice and growing up during the Depression. *To Kill a Mockingbird* garnered two Academy Awards.

Gregory Peck stars as Atticus Finch, a quiet widower and principled attorney who agrees to defend a black man named Tom Robinson (Brock Peters), falsely accused of raping a white woman. The story is told through the eyes of Finch's daughter, Jean Louise, or, as she is more commonly called, Scout (Mary Badham).

Scout, her brother Jem (Philip Alford), (and occasionally an out-of-town friend named Dill Harris, played by John Megna), come face to face with the ugliness of racism as they watch an all-white jury convict the innocent man. In the course of the trial, the children begin to see their father in a new and different light.

Though there is no mention of God in this movie, godly principles are clearly evident in the life of Atticus. He has an impact on his community because of his great character traits: fairness, forgiveness, compassion, and mercy.

Suggestions for Viewing

This classic film ought to be viewed in its entirety. However, for those who cannot find time for a full screening, try these scenes that capture the drama and message of *To Kill a Mockingbird:*

The opening scene (five or ten minutes) that settles you into the Depression era, sleepy South and introduces the main characters.

The touching scene in which a very naive Scout asks her dad why he's defending Tom, and Atticus explains his principles.

The courtroom scene (after the jury has returned a "guilty" verdict) where the blacks in the balcony stand to show their respect for Atticus as he exits.

The scene where Atticus and Jem visit Tom's family to inform them that Tom has been killed trying to escape from the sheriff's deputies.

Warning: The racial slur "nigger" is used in this movie. Audiences should be prepared for this in advance.

Important Scenes and/or Quotes

1. As Atticus stands for what is right (i.e. defending the innocent Tom), he is both loved and reviled.

   The respect he has is dramatically illustrated as Atticus departs the courtroom. A member of Tom's family chides Scout:

   "Miss Jean Louise. Miss Jean Louise. Stand up! Your father is passing by."

2. The hatred directed at Atticus Finch is best seen when Atticus and Jem drive out to Tom's house to inform his family that, "There isn't going to be any appeal. Not now. Tom is dead."

   Meeting them there is a drunken Mr. Ewell (James Anderson), the father of the alleged rape victim, and, we are led to believe, the one who actually attacked her.

   The inebriated man approaches Atticus in front of all (including Jem), glares at him in disgust and then spits in his face. Atticus wipes off the spit and walks away.

3. In another powerful moment, a neighbor tells Jem:

   "Jem, I don't know if it'll help, but I wanna say this to you. There's some men in this world who are born to do our unpleasant jobs for us. Your father is one of them."

All of these scenes demonstrate the depth of character of Atticus Finch.

Discussion Questions

How would you rate Atticus Finch as a father? As a lawyer? As a neighbor? Why?

What quality do you most admire in Atticus Finch? Why?

This movie seems to suggest that prejudice is inevitable. What, if anything, can be done to lessen racism in your community? At your school? How can we become less prejudiced in our own lives?

When Mr. Ewell spits in the face of Atticus, the lawyer "turns the other cheek" and walks away. What do you think he felt at that moment and how do you think he was able to keep from retaliating? How might *you* react in a similar situation?

What *should* you say/what *would* you say to someone who has been treated unjustly?

Outline of Talk or Wrap-up

Option #1: The Kind of Character that Impacts Others

Integrity—You're the same all the time: no hypocrisy, no skeletons in your closet, no cutting ethical or moral corners (Ps. 15).

Maturity—You stop acting like a child and start acting like a grownup (1 Cor. 13:11; Eph. 4:15).

Patience—You don't get irritated at circumstances and people when they don't go or act your way. You choose instead to trust the Lord's timing (Col. 1:11).

Acceptance—You don't demand that people be a certain way; rather, you take them as they are and love them unconditionally (Rom. 15:7).

Compassion—Your heart goes out to those in need and you provide help wherever possible (Col. 3:12).

Trustworthiness—When you say you'll do something, you do it. You are known as one who keeps his or her word (Prov. 20:6).

Option #2: Reasons Racism Is Wrong

1. We are all created in the image of God and descend from common ancestors (Gen. 1:27-29).

2. God cares more about our insides than our outside (1 Sam. 16:7; Rom. 2:11; Eph. 6:9; Col. 3:25).
3. God loves the whole world (John 3:16).
4. Heaven will be inhabited by people from "every tribe and language and people and nation" (Rev. 5:9).

Related Bible References

In discussing character, the best passages are probably Galatians 5:22–23 (the fruit of the Spirit); Ephesians 4:25—5:11; Romans 12:9–21; and Colossians 3:12–16. If you opt for a meeting on prejudice/racism, consider Jesus' treatment of the Samaritan woman (John 4), or Peter's relationship with Cornelius (Acts 10—11).

Other Ideas

Use any or all of the "Boo Radley" scenes from To Kill a Mockingbird to launch a discussion about rumors.

Len Woods

69
To Sir With Love

- PG
- 105 minutes
- A 1967 film

Synopsis and Review

In this movie examining the problems and fears of adolescence, Sidney Poitier plays a novice teacher, Mark Thackeray, who faces a class of rowdy teenagers. Mr. Thackeray is an out-of-work engineer who turns to teaching in London's East End. The senior class sets out to destroy him by breaking his spirit just as they did his predecessor. But Thackeray, no stranger to hostility, meets their challenge head-on and treats them as young adults.

Although this movie is similar to an earlier Poitier film, *Blackboard Jungle,* and is from the 60s, it is still relevant. Once the viewer gets past the dated styles and fads, he or she will see that teenagers are really not that much different today. *Sir* gives a great example of what you can become when there is someone who believes in you and refuses to give up on you. The final scene where the students show their appreciation to Thackeray for helping them grow is inspiring and moving.

Suggestions for Viewing

Sir is well worth the time spent watching the entire movie. It is possible to just use a few scenes, but the impact will be lessened. The key scene occurs at the end where the students thank Mr. Thackeray for all he has done. In the title song, "To Sir, with Love," they express their gratitude and love. It might be helpful to your discussion to have the words to the song written out.

Important Scenes and/or Quotes

The final scene takes place at the graduation party. One of the students invites Thackeray to dance. As he finally drops some of his guard and loosens up, he begins to realize how much the students have taught him in addition to his teaching them. After the dance, they call for quiet and they tell "Sir" (Thackeray) that they have a surprise for him. One of the girls sings a song that tells of their appreciation of his efforts in helping them grow up. Then they give him a present. Thackeray is moved to tears, he stumbles over his words of thanks, and leaves quickly.

Discussion Questions

Describe a situation that you have experienced that is similar to the one we just saw.

Who is the "Sir" in your life? How have you shown appreciation for him or her?

Why is it so hard to show appreciation?

When is it easy to show appreciation?

What kinds of things do you appreciate?

When have you done something good for someone and not been thanked? How did it feel?

In what ways has God helped you?

How have you shown your appreciation to God for all he has done for you?

How do you think he would like to be thanked?

Outline of Talk or Wrap-up

Start by talking about how we are dependent on others from birth to death. Eventually we go from taker to giver only to become takers again as we are older. That is the life process. How much we give or take is our choice. When we begin to appreciate the giving of others we are able to be givers ourselves.

Talk about how a thankful response to a gift can bring about a desire to offer more. There is just as much value and joy in being the giver as the receiver. Unfortunately, most of that is lost when we don't respond.

God wants us to give thanks to him for the way he has blessed us and helped us grow. We must realize that everything we have or have accomplished is from him. Being thankful cleanses us and helps us to keep our perspective right. Help your kids think of ways to thank God. Think of ways that go beyond prayer and move into action.

Related Bible References

1 Thessalonians 3:9, 5:8; 2 Thessalonians 1:3; Psalm 92:1, 100:4; Ephesians 1:16, 5:20; 1 Corinthians 15:57; 1 Timothy 4:4.

Other Ideas

Challenge your group to show appreciation to someone in their lives. Challenge them to do it in an unusual way. As a group, create a service of thanksgiving to God. Again, be creative.

Tim and Patty Atkins

70
The Trip to Bountiful

- PG
- 105 minutes
- A 1985 film

Synopsis and Review

The Trip to Bountiful is a story about an elderly woman, Mrs. Watts (Geraldine Page), who lives in Houston and whose goal is to return to her hometown, Bountiful.

She is living in a cramped city apartment with her son, Ludie Watts (John Heard) and his wife, Jessie Mae (Carlin Glynn). The two women get on each other's nerves continually. Mrs. Watts spends a great deal of her time singing old hymns, a habit that irritates her daughter-in-law.

Mrs. Watts hates living in the city—her only desire is to pay one final visit to her hometown of Bountiful. Her son and daughter-in-law don't want her to go and even try to stop her.

When she attempts to leave on the train, they try to head her off. Because the train no longer goes to Bountiful, Mrs. Watts takes the bus; as a result, her son can't stop her.

One of the delightful parts of the movie is the conversation between Mrs. Watts and a young woman named Thelma (Rebecca DeMornay) whom she meets on the bus. As they share memories and stories, Mrs. Watts opens up and is very entertaining.

When Mrs. Watts finally arrives in Bountiful, she is confronted by a hometown that is rundown and basically deserted. Yet, she is able to relive her dream as she walks the streets and revisits her farm.

As Mrs. Watts leaves, she remarks that because she has

been to Bountiful she has gained the strength that will enable her to live, even in the big city that she hates.

Suggestions for Viewing

To get the full effect of *Bountiful,* it is best to view the film in its entirety. *Bountiful* is very wholesome and contains no offensive scenes.

Important Scenes and/or Quotes

The ending to *Bountiful* is powerful. With an introduction to why Mrs. Watts wants to go back home, you could pick up the last scene on her visit. The movie ends with the hymn, "Softly and Tenderly."

The film could lead to a good discussion of the feelings of older people, the loneliness of old age, how we treat the elderly among us, and even the town of Bountiful as symbolic of someone's personal pilgrimage to the cross.

Discussion Questions

What was Mrs. Watts feeling in her son's home?

Why did she want to go back to Bountiful?

Why didn't her son and daughter-in-law want her to go?

What do you think the trip to Bountiful represents?

What did Mrs. Watts feel when she saw her old home town and house?

Why was the trip to Bountiful so beneficial for Mrs. Watts?

How can visiting the past give us power to live in the present?

What can we learn from "going back"?

As Christians, what past events have changed our lives?

How can we "live in the past" while "living in the present"?

Outline of Talk or Wrap-up

In the Bible, you find something that seems somewhat redundant. The authors tell the same story again and again. This occurs in Exodus, Numbers, Deuteronomy, and even in Acts.

What is occurring is a kind of trip to Bountiful, a pilgrimage to the reality of the past. The biblical writers are trying to get their readers to remember what it was like before they experienced God. And they are trying to get them to remember God's awesome miracles.

This kind of returning to yesterday can provide great energy for living for today. Mrs. Watts experienced this when she returned to her hometown. As she says at the end of the movie, now that she has been to Bountiful she has power to live again.

In Romans, the apostle Paul tells us that because of our belief in the death and resurrection of Christ, we are no longer to be fearful, cringing slaves but we are to be sons of God. And as sons of God, we have the power of God with us as we live. Going back to that historical event—Christ's death, once for all—frees us to live today.

Related Bible References

Acts 7—Stephen's speech to the Sanhedrin; Psalm 105; Exodus 32:13—Moses' cry to God to remember Abraham, Isaac and Israel; Exodus 8—a reminder not to forget the Lord; Romans 5–8.

Bob Arnold

71

The Verdict

- R
- 128 minutes
- A 1982 film

Synopsis and Review

Frank Galvin (Paul Newman) is a lawyer whose career is going down the tubes fast. Several events conspired to send him into a lengthy tailspin. Once a promising young attorney, now he's a drunken ambulance chaser. He has one case: a malpractice suit against a hospital and two doctors whose negligence caused a young woman to go into a coma and then a persistent vegetative state. It's a solid case, and the hospital is anxious to settle out of court; they've offered a substantial sum of money to the victim's family. Of course he should take the money (or at least his third of it) and run, but. . . . But then we wouldn't have the basis for the plot of *The Verdict*.

A funny thing happens on Frank's way to collect the settlement. He sits in the perpetual care facility where the young woman is being kept, taking a few snapshots to bolster his case. But instead of visions of dollar signs, he can't help but see this poor woman, her suffering and wasted life, and he is profoundly affected. So instead of doing what in reality most of us would have done—take the money—he decides to try the case and attempt to bring the hospital and the doctors to justice. Against all odds, he wins—but not without a lot of interesting twists.

Other cast members include Charlotte Rampling as Laura Fischer; Jack Warden as Mickey Morrissey; and James Mason as Ed Concannon.

Suggestions for Viewing

The Verdict is a well-done, tightly-wrapped drama. Paul Newman won an Oscar for his portrayal of Galvin. Unfortunately, however, there's too much profanity and suggestive sexual material in this film to show it in its entirety. After you preview, I suggest showing the scenes described below.

Important Scenes and/or Quotes

Just over ten minutes into the movie, Frank visits the victim in the perpetual care facility. This is a touching scene and gives the grim picture of what her life has become. If your kids have ever visited such a facility, this scene will hit close to home.

Around the twenty-three-minute mark we see Galvin's turning point, his second visit to the care unit. There he decides not to settle the matter out of court. Following this is his meeting with the Archbishop (the hospital where the botched operation occurred is a Catholic hospital) and his assistant, where Galvin tells them of his decision not to take their money. At approximately twenty-eight minutes, he makes the statement, "If I take the money, I'm lost." The reason for that statement is the moral crux of the movie.

The other scene that is important to your understanding of the film comes at one hour, forty-eight minutes, when Kaitlin Costello Price (Lindsay Crouse) takes the witness stand. It is a riveting scene, and pulls the pieces of what happened in the operating room together.

Discussion Questions

More than anything else, this movie is a morality play. It centers around ethics—medical ethics, legal ethics, family ethics, work ethics. The transformation of Frank Galvin from a broken, shameless, ambulance-chasing drunk to a man gripped by a higher purpose is the engine that drives this film. Ask questions like:

What makes Galvin so disgusting at the start of the movie?
The lawsuit focuses on the failure of two doctors to apply the anesthetic properly to a pregnant woman, resulting in her

becoming comatose and then lapsing into a persistent vegetative state. Doctors are human beings. Why do we hold
them accountable for mistakes like this?

Why does Galvin make the comment: "If I take the money,
I'm lost"? In what sense would he be "lost"? How does not
taking their money "redeem" him?

If you had been one of the nurses or other people assisting in
the botched operation, and you knew what actually happened—the doctors messed up in a monumental way
—what would you have done? Would you have kept quiet?
Blown the whistle? Or what?

If you had been on the jury for this case, how would you
have voted? Why?

[This question is not central to the movie, but might prove
interesting nonetheless. But use discretion in asking about
this because someone in your group may have had a similar experience.] If it were your sister (or brother or any
other loved one) in a persistent vegetative state, what do
you think you would do? Would you stay close by so you
could visit her as often as possible? Would you want to get
away from the situation? How would you deal with that
kind of tragedy?

Outline of Talk or Wrap-up

Again, this is a movie about morality, ethics, integrity, and
motivation. It makes a strong statement that there is something
more important than money. Since this may be a pretty radical
concept for most of your kids, you may have to reinforce this
several times in different ways. Some possible approaches
include: (1) God vs. mammon (Matt. 6:19–24); (2) the story of
the rich young man (Matt. 19:16–26); (3) the parable of the rich
fool (Luke 12:13-21); (4) the parable of the rich man and
Lazarus, the beggar (Luke 16:19–31).

Although it is not the main theme of *The Verdict,* there is a
less prominent motif of defending the defenseless, i.e. the
comatose woman. Galvin, in effect, becomes her advocate as
well as her family's. Consider stoking the fires of latent idealism
that most young people have by discussing this theme and
examining some of the many passages in Scripture that deal

with it: Leviticus 25:35–43; Deuteronomy 15:4–8; Psalm 12:5; 82:1–4; Isaiah 1:16–17; James 1:27.

Related Bible References

See above.

Other Ideas

It would probably be very enlightening to invite a doctor and a lawyer to discuss the relative merits of some of the issues raised in *The Verdict*. Be sure you think through what you want to have come out of this discussion with both (or all) participants ahead of time, so that your program produces some light as well as heat.

Kent Keller

72

Witness

- R
- 112 minutes
- A 1985 film

Synopsis and Review

Witness is the story of Philadelphia police detective John
Book's (Harrison Ford) encounter with the Amish culture of
Pennsylvania. This film depicts the stark contrast between
the private, unmodernized, and religious culture of the
Amish community and the open, modern, and secular cul-
ture of an American city.

Following the funeral of her husband, Rachel Lapp
(Kelly McGillis) and her son Samuel (Lukas Haas) set out for
Baltimore to visit her sister. Traveling by Amtrak, they have
a three-hour wait in the Philadelphia train station. In the
station's restroom, young Samuel witnesses the brutal murder of an undercover narcotics officer. Consequently Samuel
becomes the primary material witness in the murder case.

In police headquarters, Samuel spots a newspaper clip-
ping with a photograph of one of the men he saw commit
the murder. It is Lt. McFee (Danny Glover), another narcotics officer on the force. As it turns out, McFee, Book's
boss Paul Schaefer (Josef Sommer), and a third narcotics
officer are somehow involved in the mysterious disappearance, four years ago, of over 500 gallons of a drug used to
make heroin. Book, not knowing about Schaefer's involvement, turns to him for help. In turn, Book becomes a target
for elimination and is subsequently shot by McFee.
Realizing Schaefer's involvement, a wounded Book unwittingly retreats, with the Lapps, into the heart of the
Pennsylvania Amish country.

The remainder of the film is an exploration of the cultural differences that Book encounters and the unraveling of the crime. Book's partner, Carter (Brent Jennings), is killed, leaving Book to stand alone against Schaefer and his cohorts. During his time with the Amish, Book becomes romantically involved with Rachel. This leaves him with the choice of abandoning the modern world—his world—or leaving behind the woman he has come to love. Eventually, Schaefer is apprehended, and Book chooses to return to Philadelphia.

Suggestions for Viewing

This film does contain some graphic violence (the murdering of the narcotics officer and the death of two of the three men trying to kill Book), and some occasionally offensive language (especially Book's final confrontation with Schaefer). It also includes a tastefully executed sponge bathing scene in which McGillis is briefly revealed nude, from the waist up. As a movie, *Witness* would be most effective shown from beginning to end. Much of what happens is visual, with the Amish country beautifully portrayed. The suspense of the plot as it builds is important to the film's impact and enjoyment. At the same time, if the scenes described above would be inappropriate for your audience there are several dynamic sequences that could be used with a plot summary as discussion starters. They are described below.

Important Scenes and/or Quotes

At the heart of *Witness* is the implicit tension between the Amish way of life into which Book has been thrust and the modern American lifestyle that he is used to. The following scenes vividly portray this cultural tension:

1. The scene where Rachel and Samuel are being taken to the police station so that Samuel can identify the murderer. In this scene Rachel tells Book, "We want nothing to do with your laws. I want no further part of this." And she tells Samuel, "We don't need to know anything about him (Book)."
2. The scene where Eli demonstrates extreme reverence for

human life as he contemplates allowing the wounded Book to stay on his farm. He says, "This is a man's life. We hold it in our hands."

3. The scene where Eli lectures Samuel about the evil nature of guns. He says, "You take into your hands. You take into your heart. Come out from among them and be ye separate."

4. The scene at the breakfast table where Book jokes, "Honey, that's great coffee," referring to a television commercial, only to be reminded by the family's silence that they don't have a television set.

Discussion Questions

What are some of the differences between the Amish and the modern American way of life?

The Bible tells us that while believers are *in* the world, they should not be *of* the world. What does that mean? How do the Amish try to obey that command?

What did Eli mean by the statement, "What you take into your hand you also take into your heart"? How might this apply to other things beside guns?

Outline of Talk or Wrap-up

The essential theme of *Witness* is the contrast between two very divergent cultures. The Amish attempt to insulate themselves from the evils of the world by totally separating themselves from it. Modern Christians, on the other hand, sometimes go to the other extreme and totally identify with the world. Use *Witness* to discuss the implications of both ways of responding as well as the biblical alternative of being salt and light in the world (Matt. 5:13–16).

Related Bible References

John 15:19; 17:14–16 (the believer's relationship with the world); James 4:4 (warning against friendship with the world); and 1 John 2:15–17 (warning against loving the things of the world).

Robert Eugene DiPaolo

73
The Wizard of Oz

- Unrated
- 102 minutes
- A 1939 film classic

Synopsis and Review

This classic 1939 tale tells the story of Dorothy who ends up in Oz after a storm and subsequent blow to the head. She and three friends take a journey to find the Wizard of Oz in hopes that he will give them their hearts' desires.

Seen by every kid in America, this movie is a great example of searching for your dreams and overcoming obstacles. The bright colors, imaginative people and wonderful music make it a movie that never loses its charm.

Characters: Dorothy (Judy Garland); Toto (Toto); Hunk/The Scarecrow (Ray Bolger); Zeke/The Cowardly Lion (Bert Lahr); Hickory/The Tin Woodsman (Jack Haley); Auntie Em (Clara Blandick); Uncle Henry (Charles Grapewin); Nasty Neighbor/Wicked Witch of the West (Margaret Hamilton); Good Witch of the North—Glinda (Billie Burke); Carnie Man/Wizard (Frank Morgan).

Suggestions for Viewing

The Wizard of Oz is compelling as a story of contentment. However, because of its popularity, viewing the entire one hundred two minutes is probably not necessary. Two scenes capture the heart of the movie. The first is the bestowal of gifts by the Wizard. The key in this scene is that those desires which Dorothy and the others sought, they already possessed.

The second scene is where Glinda tells Dorothy how to get home.

Important Scenes and/or Quotes

The following dialogue is where Glinda tells Dorothy how to get back to Kansas.

Glinda:	You don't need to be helped any longer. You've always had the power to go back to Kansas.
Dorothy:	I have?
Scarecrow:	Then why didn't you tell her before?
Glinda:	Because she wouldn't have believed me. She had to learn it for herself.
Scarecrow:	What have you learned, Dorothy?
Dorothy:	Well, I think that it wasn't enough just to see Uncle Henry and Auntie Em, and that if I go looking for my heart's desire again, I won't go any further than my own backyard. Because if it isn't there I never really lost it to begin with. Isn't that right?
Glinda:	That's all it is.
Scarecrow:	But it's so easy. I should have thought of it for her.
Tin Man:	I should have felt it in my heart.
Glinda:	No, she had to find out for herself.

Discussion Questions
Learning the Truth

Describe Glinda's teaching style.

Why would Glinda want Dorothy to discover the truth for herself?

What important truths have you learned that way?

How were you taught manners? Social behavior? Academics? Christianity?

Which way would you rather be taught?

What was Jesus' style of teaching?

Heart's Desires

What are some of your heart's desires?

What does Dorothy mean that if it's not in your own backyard, then you've never lost it?

What does Glinda mean when she says, "That's all it is"?

When do you feel God helping you find your desires?

Outline of Talk or Wrap-up

The wrap-up for this video could take one of two directions. The first is the idea that learning has more meaning when the student has discovered truth for himself or herself. Then the student fully believes in it. The implication of this for evangelism is tremendous. Too often we spend our time expounding truth and laying out laws. The amazing thing is that when someone even briefly experiences God's truth, he or she will fully know and own God's love.

The second direction would be dealing with the fulfilling of our heart's desires. God truly wants to give us our heart's desires. Use biblical examples of God working in the lives of believers. Often, we spend too much time looking for what we already have instead of appreciating what we have and using it. When we strive to use the gifts and abilities that God has given us, our desires are not only fulfilled, they expand. When our desires are compatible with God's desires for us, our potential is limitless.

Related Bible References

Psalm 37:4; Philippians 4:19; Revelation 3:17; Psalm 145:16; Hebrews 11:16; Matthew 6:8; Micah 7:3.

Tim and Patty Atkins

74
Yentl

- PG
- 134 minutes
- A 1983 film

Synopsis and Review

Yentl, set in eastern Europe in the early 1900s, considers the roles of men and women. The preface to the movie begins, "In a time when the world of study belonged only to men, there lived a girl called Yentl."

Yentl is a young Jewish woman who wants to study the Talmud. Young Jewish women, she is told, learn to cook and get married. Yentl does not want to cook and get married. Though forbidden, Yentl's father, a rabbi, secretly gives her lessons in the Talmud.

After her father's death, Yentl cuts her hair and leaves her hometown. Pretending to be a boy, she enters a Yeshiva (a school for young Jewish men) to formally study the Talmud. Though no one guesses her true identity, she falls in love with her new best friend, another Yeshiva student, Avidore.

When Avidore is scorned by the family of the girl he loves, Yentl reluctantly (because he begs her) agrees to marry his fiance, Haddas (Amy Irving). Haddas is the antithesis to Yentl in many ways. She loves to cook, she is ready to serve her husband, she has no interest in Talmud, she remains quiet until spoken to. But both women have fallen in love with Avidore.

Finally, Yentl can no longer continue the charade. Haddas patiently waits for her to consummate their new marriage (which, of course, Yentl cannot do), and Avidore still desperately loves Haddas. Yentl feels compelled to reveal her true identity. Avidore is stunned and angered but ultimately shakes his head and wonders how he ever could have thought Yentl was a man.

Quietly, after writing the local rabbi to declare the marriage void, Yentl leaves for New York, where women are given more freedom.

Suggestions for Viewing

Yentl is just over two hours long. Nothing in it is offensive (though there is a brief back shot of Avidore running naked into a lake). At times the action drags, especially during some of the songs.

Important Scenes and/or Quotes

1. A seller of books has come to Yentl's village. He has study books for the men and other books for the women. Yentl attempts to buy a study book.

   Seller: Story books for women. Study books for men. Picture books for women.
   Yentl: Why?
   Seller: It is written.
   Yentl: Where?

2. As Yentl and her father study one night, Yentl asks, "Where is it written what I was meant to be?"
3. Yentl and Avidore are walking by a river one day discussing Haddas.

   Avidore: She's a girl in love, what do you expect?
   Yentl: She doesn't say very much does she?
   Avidore: What does she have to say?
   Yentl: Don't you ever wonder what she is thinking?
   Avidore: No! What could she be thinking? I don't need her to think.

As they continue walking they come across a woman breast-feeding her child. Avidore exclaims, "Can you do that? Create life, give birth to sons? When you can do that then you tell me we are equal!"

Discussion Questions

How did people respond when Yentl said she wanted to study the Talmud? Why was their response so strong?

What are some of the differences between men and women? Or are they exactly alike but in different types of bodies?

What does the Bible say about the roles of men and women? In the home? In church? What are some specific passages? Do you agree with the Bible? Why or why not?

Why do you think God made men and women so different? Do you think he really had a specific reason or that he just made us that way?

If God has made man and woman specifically the way he did would you agree that the most satisfying way to live, then, would be to "celebrate" whatever sex you happen to be? Or is it legitimate for a woman to fill the role given to man and a man to fill the role of woman?

Outline of Talk or Wrap-up

Yentl explores the roles of men and women. Although the film is set in eastern Europe at the turn of the century, the questions it raises are universal. Use *Yentl* to promote discussion on the roles of men and women.

Explain that God has created us differently. He did that for a purpose. Both males and females can find their greatest joy in living fully the role that God has set, not in defining their own.

Make it clear that these roles cannot be discovered by tradition, or innovation, or even what people think the Bible teaches. Only a clear understanding of the principles of Scripture can determine what the roles are. Emphasize that various roles do not in any way change the worth of an individual.

Related Bible References

Genesis 2 (creation of Adam and Eve), 3 (the fall); Proverbs 31:10–31 (noble wife); Romans 1:26–27 (homosexuality); Ephesians 5:22–33 (husbands and wives), 1 Timothy 2:9–15 (church), Galations 3:26–29 (equality).

Other Ideas

Yentl could be used in a discussion on the difference between tradition and the truth of the Bible. Many of the answers Yentl heard had no basis but tradition. Those answers are not good enough.

Jared Reed

75
Zelig

- PG
- 84 minutes
- A 1983 film

Synopsis and Review

Zelig is a Woody Allen film, made to resemble a news documentary of the 40s. It is about a man who conforms physically to be like those around him. For example, when he is sitting next to a Chinese man, he develops Chinese characteristics. If he is sitting next to a fat man, he suddenly becomes obese.

Filmed in black and white, *Zelig* tells the story of Leonard Zelig (Woody Allen) and psychologist Dr. Eudora Fletcher's (Mia Farrow) efforts to cure him. It is definitely pure Woody Allen and a bit off the wall. All in all, it is a highly creative look at our need to conform to the world around us.

Suggestions for Viewing

Most audiences may find *Zelig* too bizarre to view in its entirety. It is very easy to understand the point of the movie by watching several of the scenes, especially those where Zelig changes to conform to his surroundings. Another important scene is where Zelig tells the psychologist why he changes like he does.

Rated PG, *Zelig* contains language that may be offensive.

Important Scenes and/or Quotes

The following is a paraphrase of Zelig's answer as to why he transforms to match those around him.

"Ever since I was a child, I've always wanted to fit in. I was afraid I wouldn't have a place to belong. I put all my effort into being like those around me. After a while, I couldn't control my transforming to where I am now. Now I don't even know who I am."

Discussion Questions

In what areas of our lives do we try to match our surroundings?

What groups of people are noted for nonconformity?

What are the dangers of conformity?

What are the dangers of nonconformity?

What makes a person want to conform?

Was Jesus a conformist or a nonconformist? Explain your answer.

Why are people afraid to be different?

How does that hinder our effectiveness as Christians?

Outline of Talk or Wrap-up

This movie is an excellent springboard to talk about peer pressure and conforming to the world's standards. Explain that although Zelig is an extreme case, we all tend to do some laughable things in the name of conformity. Use fashion and fads as an example. We conform because it is easier and safer, and we want to fit in.

Illustrate examples of Jesus' nonconformity. Explain that as Christians we are called to be different from the world. Finally, point out that God loves us for who we really are, not for how well we fit into the group.

Related Bible References

Romans 8:28; 2 Corinthians 1:24; Ephesians 5:1; Romans 12:1–2; 1 Corinthians 11:1; Ephesians 4:20–24; 1 Corinthians 16:13; 3 John 11.

Tim and Patty Atkins